SCOTNOTE
Number 3.

CW00661326

Sue Glover's

Bondagers

and

The Straw Chair

John Hodgart

Association for Scottish Literary Studies 2012

Published by
Association for Scottish Literary Studies
Scottish Literature
7 University Gardens
University of Glasgow
Glasgow G12 8QH
www.asls.org.uk

ASLS is a registered charity no. SC006535

First published 2012

A CIP catalogue for this title
is available from the British Library

ISBN 978-1-906841-12-6

The Association for Scottish Literary Studies
acknowledges the support of Creative Scotland
towards the publication of this book.

ALBA | CHRUTHACHAIL

CONTENTS

SCOTNOTES

Study guides to major Scottish writers and literary texts

Produced by the Education Committee
of the Association for Scottish Literary Studies

THE ASSOCIATION FOR SCOTTISH LITERARY STUDIES aims to promote the study, teaching and writing of Scottish literature, and to further the study of the languages of Scotland.

To these ends, the ASLS publishes works of Scottish literature; literary criticism and in-depth reviews of Scottish books in *Scottish Literary Review*; short articles, features and news in *ScotLit*; and scholarly studies of language in *Scottish Language*. It also publishes *New Writing Scotland*, an annual anthology of new poetry, drama and short fiction, in Scots, English and Gaelic. ASLS has also prepared a range of teaching materials covering Scottish language and literature for use in schools.

All the above publications are available as a single 'package', in return for an annual subscription. Enquiries should be sent to:

ASLS
Scottish Literature
7 University Gardens
University of Glasgow
Glasgow G12 8QH

Tel/fax +44 (0)141 330 5309
e-mail **office@asls.org.uk**
or visit our website at **www.asls.org.uk**

Both plays are available in one volume in
Methuen's *Modern Plays* series (first published 1997).

1. SUE GLOVER'S PLAYS

Sue Glover was born in Edinburgh in 1943 where she grew up and attended university. She began writing plays for the radio in the 1970s, making her stage debut at the Little Lyceum in 1980 with *The Seal Wife*, her first full-length play, in which many of the recurring features and concerns of her work are to be found: the influence of oral culture and folklore, the re-examination of history, legend and myth from a female perspective, giving voice to marginalised, exploited or alienated women whose identity has been defined by their domestic role or social status in a patriarchal society. The themes of alienation and marginalisation are also explored in *An Island in Largo* (1981), a play inspired by Daniel Defoe's *Robinson Crusoe*, which examines Alexander Selkirk's alienation from his own society on his return home, a theme which she recently revisited in a short play, *Bear on a Chain* for Oran Mor, Glasgow (2010). Glover's exploration of history and mythology often portrays a hypocritical male-dominated society and its institutions as repressive and corrosive influences not only on female identity, but on human nature as a whole, issues explored further in *The Bubble Boy* (1981), *The Straw Chair* (1988), *Bondagers* (1990) and *Sacred Hearts* (1994) which deals with the occupation of a Glasgow church by a group of five prostitutes to protest about their lack of protection from the predations of a serial killer. In contrast, *Shetland Saga* (2000) depicts the hostility faced by a group of Bulgarian sailors stranded in a Shetland harbour, while *Marilyn* (2011) explores the relationship between two icons of twentieth century cinema, Marilyn Monroe and Simone Signoret, and their contrasting struggles to escape the mythology of their celluloid fame and discover who they really are. Several of her plays have been translated and produced in Europe and North America. Her television work includes *The Home Front, The Bubble Boy, The Spaver Connection, Dear Life, Mrs Miller and Madame Montand* and work for *Take the High Road* and *Strathblair*. *Bondagers* which won the London Weekend Television Plays on Stage Award (1990) has been hailed as a modern Scottish

1

classic and is included in Canongate's anthology, *Twentieth Century Scottish Drama*.

Glover's work needs to be set in the context of a very strong tradition of modern Scottish feminist drama which includes the work of Ena Lamont Stewart, Joan Ure, Liz Lochhead, Rona Munro, Ann Marie di Mambro, Sharman Macdonald and others.

2. DEPICTING THE PEASANTRY IN SCOTTISH LITERATURE

Even although most of Victorian and early twentieth century Scottish literature is set in the countryside or small towns and villages, it is often very nostalgic or sentimental (the popular 'Kailyard School' of fiction) avoiding the harsher realities of rural life, with a few notable exceptions. As far as the theatre is concerned, apart from the music hall, a native tradition of Scottish drama struggled to emerge until well into the twentieth century, for many political, economic and cultural reasons, such as the kirk's disapproval or the power and prestige of English at the expense of Scots.

In the five years before the First World War the Glasgow Repertory Theatre did much to encourage the emergence of native Scottish plays, including Donald Colquhoun's *Jean* (1910), in which we see a realistic presentation of a small farmer's struggle to survive, while John Brandane's Hebridean play, *The Glen is Mine* (1925) examines the conflict between development and conservation and raises important questions about the future of the Highlands. Although homely Scots plays of the emerging amateur stage from the 1920s and 1930s onwards are often set in an older rural or historical Scotland, they are mainly nostalgic and pawky comedies.

Apart from historical dramas, serious Scottish plays from around the Second World War onwards turned more towards the harsh realities and injustices of urban industrial society, such as the Clydeside plays of the 1930s and 1940s or the revival of political and polemic dramas by the 7:84 Theatre Company and Wildcat in the 1970s and 1980s. By contrast, plays dealing with the lives of the non-industrial working classes have been very few indeed. The most memorable of these were *The Cheviot, the Stag and the Black Black Oil* by John McGrath (1973) which focuses on the Clearances and the issue of land ownership, and Donald Campbell's *The Widows of Clyth* (1979) which depicts the suffering of a nineteenth-century Caithness fishing community. Probably the only drama depicting what it actually feels like to work

3

on the land has been an adaptation of a novel – Lewis Grassic Gibbon's *Sunset Song*, which has been performed several times during the past two decades.

Nevertheless, Scottish theatre, such as it was before the twentieth century, produced at least one great rural drama: Alan Ramsay's *The Gentle Shepherd* (1725), which remained hugely popular well into the next century. Ramsay's verse drama, with songs, is based on the very fashionable pastoral tradition about the simple lives and loves of innocent peasants, set in an Arcadian fairytale world, something that goes back a long way in European literature to classical times. Although Ramsay deploys many features of the fairytale, he also satirises the pastoral genre through his use of a real Scottish setting, earthy rustic language, comic realism and above all convincingly true-to-life shepherds and shepherdesses whose love lives are full of complications. Possibly Glover is paying tribute to Ramsay by giving Sara's partner, Patie, the same name as Ramsay's hero.

Until *Bondagers* (1990) – about 265 years later – the real working life and culture of rural Scotland has been markedly absent from our professional stage. *Bondagers* is arguably the first Scottish play to make us really see, feel and smell what it is like to face a life of never-ending toil with the land and the seasons. Yet we have a very rich tradition of dramatic poems, stories and songs about rural life which were a vital part of a communal culture, especially the oral tradition, often dealing very realistically and humorously with the toils or troubles of peasant folk, as well as their fun and festivals. This tradition echoes down through *Bondagers* via the use of folk songs, dances, superstitions and celebrations.

Perhaps in this context we also need to consider what was still regarded almost as a sacred text by many Scots of a previous generation – Burns' poem 'The Cottar's Saturday Night' which venerated the lives of the poor but 'noble peasant'. In this poem Burns presents us with a hugely idealised picture of a virtuous, obedient rural peasantry worshipping God under the eye of a strict but benign patriarch – quite the opposite of the harsh reality depicted in *Bondagers*. In contrast to Burns, Sue Glover deliberately focuses on the lives of women, with men only 'appearing' offstage and male behaviour and male authority revealed as foolish, uncaring or destructive.

Sunset Song by Lewis Grassic Gibbon also casts a powerful shadow over Glover's play and, in fact, there are many interesting points of comparison between the two works. Although Gibbon's classic was written in the early 1930s, it is set about forty to fifty years later than *Bondagers*, but it also depicts the never-ending toil of farm work and we can even see a similar love–hate relationship with the land in both the life of Gibbon's heroine, Chris Guthrie, and the women in Glover's play. Indeed, one of Glover's main characters, Liza, has several things in common with Chris: a fierce father; a loving mother; a brother who emigrates, leaving her on her own, an orphan, but a proudly independent young woman who loves and loses someone.

While Liza, like Chris, loves and hates the land, she does not, however, have the sort of dominating central importance or symbolic status that Gibbon gives his heroine. There are even parallels between Meg Menzies, the heroine of Gibbon's short story 'Smeddum', and Maggie, the harassed hind's wife and mother of a very large brood of bairns.

Whereas *Bondagers* concentrates on a band of female labourers during one farming year, leaving all the men offstage, *Sunset Song* is centred on the life of a tenant farmer's daughter and it deals with the profound changes in the lives of the whole community as a result of the First World War, thus covering a much longer time span. Yet both works also offer a longer perspective on human relationship with the land by depicting a character who is in tune with the past and can see 'ghosts' but can also perhaps envisage what will happen in the future. *Bondagers,* however, does not share Gibbon's theory of a 'golden age' of human freedom and innocence before the enslavement and corruption of civilisation, or offer any vision or dream of its recreation.

3. BONDAGERS

Introduction
At first glance a play about nineteenth-century women farm workers might seem to hold little relevance or appeal to 21st century students, yet *Bondagers* is a powerful and moving drama about a band of brave, vulnerable women struggling to survive hardship, exploitation and injustice, while it also celebrates the human strengths and loyalties that help them cope with their bondage to a way of life that they both love and hate.

First and foremost it is a very authentic and unsentimental portrayal of the lives of our rural ancestors who battled with a hard and unjust world and passed on not just their genes and survival skills, but also something of their humanity, culture and language. Unfortunately their orally transmitted folk knowledge has often been forgotten or dismissed by the modern world, thereby disinheriting us from an essential source of shared human skills and wisdom, rooted in a deep understanding of the natural world, social co-operation and interdependence.

In addition to this it is a timeless drama about the suffering of poor women the world over, enduring the perennial pains of love, loss and longing. Perhaps we should also reflect on the fact that probably a majority of the world's population still struggles to make a living from the land, especially in poorer countries and that even the affluent parts of the world depend on the cheap and often exploited labour of peasant men and women for many of the raw materials, commodities and luxuries we take for granted.

Yet at a deeper level *Bondagers* is also a play about human identity and direction, about our relationship to the land itself and to each other, exploring the primeval conflict between the restless nomadic, possibly male, desire to move on and seek a better life elsewhere and the ancient tribal longing, possibly female, to put down deeper roots and find a sense of belonging to a place we can call 'home'. Thus it is partly about how our lives have been affected by past lives and what we can learn from them, but it also asks some searching questions

6

about 'progress' and the future and surely that is important and well worth studying.

It might also be interesting to compare *Bondagers* with another play, *The Steamie* by Tony Roper, which celebrates the bonds a group of 1950s Glasgow women share while doing their families' washing at Hogmanay. If you have read *Men Should Weep* by Ena Lamont Stewart, a play about poverty in Glasgow during the 1930s, you might also draw quite a few parallels with another Maggie, the mother of a very large family and central character in that play.

Setting and structure

As Sue Glover points out in her prefatory note, bondagers were 'the women workers of the great Border farms' and a hind was a farm worker 'hired on the condition that he brought a female worker to work alongside him', someone he had to lodge and feed alongside his own family in a tiny farm cottage. (See the famous painting *A Hind's Daughter* by Sir James Guthrie, 1883.) In *Bondagers*, Maggie dreams of a better house with a roof that does not leak, while the women discuss their situation in Act One, Scene Ten and agitation for change is also referred to several times, especially the maister's political activities. They lived in an extremely unequal society in which bondagers were fairly close to the bottom. In contrast to this, Steenie's letter from Canada in Act Two, Scene Seven seems like a message from another planet where there are as yet no masters or class structure, a country that is 'good if a man keeps his health'.

Glover sets the play in 1860, at the height of the Victorian age, a time of dramatic change and transition from an agrarian to a predominantly urban industrial society, with new farming methods and increased mechanisation leading to severe rural unemployment and migration to the city. As Glover says in her introduction, there have been more agricultural advances in the last two hundred than in the last eight thousand years.

Both the time frame of the narrative and plot structure revolve around the cycle of the farm workers' year from the hiring fair in February to the same event one year later as we follow a series of episodes in the lives of a group of women working together on one Border farm. Act One begins with the uncertainties of one hiring fair and takes us through that summer to the climax of the farming year at the Autumn harvest kirn, while Act Two begins at Hogmanay and ends with the uncertainty facing the women as they move on to another hiring fair one year later.

Since the play follows the cycle of the year, ending almost where it began, the play could be said to have a circular structure which is appropriate to the time frame and the theme. Glover is also very selective about the particular parts of the year around which the central dramatic action revolves as the bondagers' year is punctuated by two important pagan festivals: the kirn or harvest home, a celebration of fertility and the fruits of toil, and Hogmanay, the old midwinter celebration of rebirth and renewal – both celebrations allowing temporary release from enslavement to a system of agrarian bondage and both playing a powerful role in the women's lives.

Although we follow the changes in the lives of her characters over one year, we are also made aware of a longer time frame operating in their lives and also a much greater time frame affecting all human life. Firstly, what happened in the past to most of her main characters is vividly recalled several times in the play, as past events and past decisions have had a powerful influence on their lives, especially Sara's inability to leave Scotland with Patie, or what we learn about Liza and Ellen whose lives are interwoven in many ways. However, we are also conscious of the shadow of an ancient past and those who have worked this land before through Tottie's vision of the ghost up on the moor (Act One, Scene Five), while a farmer of the future offers a chilling vision of a land without folk (Act Two, Scene Two). Thus we are presented with a long-term perspective on human 'progress' and our changing relationship to the land over millennia.

Plot
Although the play uses an episodic structure, in many respects the plot follows the classical structure of exposition, conflict, crisis, climax and conclusion, but Glover also undermines this

as she deliberately sets up conflicts and patterns of expectation which do not really lead to the play's dramatic climax. Indeed nothing turns out quite as expected or as anticipated by anyone and that is a key element in the plot and also the theme of the work. In the very opening scene, once individual characters emerge from the anonymous 'crowd' at the hiring fair, we firstly focus on Liza who stands out from the crowd because of her proud and independent spirit, and then we notice the awkward and anxious mother–daughter pair of Sara and Tottie, then thirdly we hear from Maggie, the hind's wife, who is anxious about everything. From the start Glover is therefore clearly directing our attention not so much to any one individual but to a whole group of women, the way of life they share and the relationships between them and clearly this remains her main focus throughout.

However, we soon see tensions and conflicts beginning to develop between the women, firstly between Liza and Maggie who is highly suspicious and perhaps jealous of youngsters like Liza and Jenny. Liza does not at first seem a very likeable character as she is unsympathetic towards the childlike Tottie and is also resentful towards the former bondager, Ellen, mainly for jilting her brother Steenie who ran off to Canada as a consequence. In contrast, the 'simpleton', Tottie, is naturally friendly and is full of admiration for Ellen, while we are also perhaps intrigued by Tottie's strange 'ghost' story and her mother's story about Tottie's father, Patie, and why Sarah couldn't go with him to Canada.

We therefore naturally expect that the character differences and tensions revealed thus far will intensify and come to a head sooner or later and once Liza and Jenny have their eyes fixed on suitable partners for the kirn, we perhaps also suspect that the young girls' love interests might form the central part of the plot, especially after their Halloween 'predictions' and the build-up to the kirn which forms the dramatic climax of Act One, just as it was the climax of the farming year. The kirn has its roots far back in harvest fertility rituals which celebrated fecundity in nature and humans, but unfortunately this is where things start to 'go wrong' as events do not at all turn out as expected. Liza does not get

her man, the 'bonnie black-eyed plooman', Kello, but instead
it is the innocent Tottie who makes herself available to him,
something that provides a very surprising and shocking end
to the first act. The very person the other girls have tried to
ignore up till now becomes a cruelly ironical harvest queen,
or, to be more accurate, a sacrificial virgin, with everyone's
attention focused on her.

The kirn is in fact the real turning point in the whole play,
a pivotal action around which lives are changed. After it
nothing is quite the same ever again, as we see the cruel
consequences of what happened that night unfold in Act Two
and realise its full impact on the lives of all those concerned.
The conflict between Liza and Maggie also intensifies after
the kirn, as Maggie blames the younger woman for what
happened to Tottie, but she also fears her husband, Andra, is
lusting after Liza and this adds to the latter's misery, especially after what Kello did at the kirn, though she is clearly
still attracted to him. Again, however, the action is not
centred on Liza's emotional turmoil, as we might expect, say,
in a love drama, but instead the play increasingly focuses
on Tottie as we see her undergoing a disturbing character
transformation as a result of having been sexually exploited
and then spurned by Kello, something that eventually has
dark and tragic consequences.

The dramatic climax of Act Two is not a lovers' separation,
quarrel or reunion, but again it is something unexpected:
Kello's accident in the barn and the dire consequences, not
just for himself but for the increasingly distraught Tottie
who is blamed, captured and incarcerated. At the end of
the play, no one's hopes are realised, there is little to look
forward to and there is no closure as everyone has to move
on once again to find a new place. Much has changed in the
women's lives during this year, but some things have not and
some things probably never will, at least for the bondagers
facing an uncertain future in a hard, cruel and unjust world
and inevitably another year on another farm at the mercy
of the weather or an unkind 'maister'. All they have is each
other and that is perhaps their greatest, in fact their only,
insurance policy in the struggle for survival.

4. CHARACTERS AND THEMES

First and foremost *Bondagers* is a play which dramatises the way of life of a whole class of working women in nineteenth-century Scotland by focusing on the struggles of one particular group, the interrelationships between them and the bonds they develop over the period of one farming year. As it focuses very much on the group as a whole there is arguably no central character in the conventional sense, although individual characters and conflicts are convincingly presented and Glover succeeds in making us very interested in how the relationships between them will develop and what will happen to each of them by the end of the play.

THE WOMEN

Liza and Maggie
Liza is perhaps the closest to becoming a central character as she develops most as a person throughout the play and she is also possibly the character with whom a young audience is most likely to identify. As we have already noted, hers is the first individual character voice we hear in the play and it is also very significant that she is given the last line in the play. At the very start she stands out from the crowd at the fair in a number of ways: she keeps herself apart from the others; she is young and pretty, independent, proud, possibly even conceited; she boasts that she'll be hired early and then lists what she will and will not do, thereby stressing how determined or choosy she is, something that earns a gentle reprimand from Sara. The others hope for things of a very practical nature, but Liza's top priority is a big farm with 'plenty lassies for the crack, plenty ploomen for the dancing', and, while the others hope for a dry day for the flitting, she plans to buy a new hat, which suggests she cares more about her appearance and having a good time than about the work, something that might make her more interesting or appealing.

Yet, while we might admire her strong independence and apparently carefree outlook, she does not at first appear a very sympathetic character, especially in her attitude towards Tottie whom she regards as 'a pest.' She even rejects Jenny's kindly offer to teach her to spin, though we soon realise that there is more to this than meets the eye as this will bring her into contact with Ellen, something she is keen to avoid. She seems to be only looking out for herself and also seems to have a bit of a chip on the shoulder which contrasts with the innocence and friendliness of Tottie and the openness and honesty of Ellen. Perhaps we might be inclined to agree that Jenny is right to call her a 'besom' at the end of Act One, Scene Four.

She is also in conflict with Maggie for much of the play. Even before Liza has met Maggie, we can anticipate that there might be friction between them because, when we hear Maggie worrying about who Andra will hire in Act One, Scene One, she says 'just as long as she takes to the bairns' and in the very next line we hear Liza saying, 'I'm not going to any place hoachin wi bairns!'. Liza is again rebuked by Sara as 'there's bound to be bairns' and indeed Maggie is burdened with around eight of them, a fairly average family size in those days. Liza is even kicked by one of Maggie's children when she first arrives and throughout the play she shows little or no interest in any of them, especially the baby, something Maggie finds incomprehensible.

Liza could, therefore, be seen as a modern type of young woman who challenges or even rejects the conventional roles and duties of marriage and motherhood which the older women are conditioned to accept unquestioningly, mainly because they do not have any choice. She also tells Maggie in no uncertain terms that she will not be sleeping with bairns, when there is really no alternative, but ironically this also reveals her naivety as she 'gapes astonished' when the more worldly-wise Jenny informs her that this is what actually keeps her safe at night from the attentions of Andra, Maggie's husband. Perhaps it is this contradiction between vociferously asserting her independence and unwittingly revealing her naivety that first leads us to see that she is not actually quite as confident and carefree as she at first seems.

In fact the conflict between the older married woman and the independent young woman is a key element in the drama and is used by Glover to examine the polar opposites of feminine experience. Maggie is suspicious and perhaps even jealous of younger women and obviously has Liza in mind when she says in Act One, Scene Ten, 'a sweet face won't shift the sharn', while she clearly resents Liza complaining about the children and the food. This argument soon develops into open conflict, especially when Liza snaps at Maggie with 'I'm not your servant!' and Maggie responds with 'I'm not your washerwoman!'.

In the following scene this conflict erupts into something much more personal, especially after Liza is dismissive of Maggie's attempts to teach her about milking and she scornfully remarks that Maggie has plenty milk of her own if the 'coo runs dry'. Liza then asserts her determination never to be burdened with lots of children and, when Maggie proudly tries to defend her role as mother of a large brood, the younger woman bites back with extremely unkind comments about why she hears Maggie crying in the night and the lengths she has to go to avoid getting pregnant again. The older woman is extremely upset and turns to the cradle to feed the baby, though it is in fact she that is being 'comforted by the nursing'. In contrast to Liza's 'insouciant, unrepentant' attitude here, Maggie is so hurt by her bitchy remarks that we probably feel far more sympathy for the older woman at this stage.

From the start we see and hear Maggie in a separate space from the bondagers, as befits her different status, but like them she is anxious about what sort of farm they will end up on, though in contrast to them she is worried about what sort of bondagers her husband will hire at the fair. Her role is that of the dutiful wife and mother who is constantly harassed, struggling to feed many mouths with no time for herself, accepting her role unquestioningly as there is really no other option for her. She is also resigned to making the best of things, often with a wry sense of humour, hoping for practical consolations like a decent master, a roof that does not leak, a dry day for the flitting and she even dreams of things eventually becoming easier for her as more of her older children start work and of course begin the whole cycle all over again.

As soon as Liza meets Maggie we sense the tension between them over the younger woman's attitude towards children, partly due to the fact that Andra has obviously lied about the number they have, something Maggie denies, but which only serves to fuel her resentment and suspicion that Liza has indeed been hired by Andra because of her pretty face. Naturally defensive of her husband and her large family, she resents Liza's unsympathetic attitude and obviously sees her as a cheeky young besom who knows little or nothing about the realities of life that lie in wait for her.

On the other hand, Maggie is also extremely strict, even judgemental in matters of sexual morality and marriage, as if she is a kind of matriarchal moral guardian.

What light do you think is shed on her character by her comments to Sara about only being hand-fasted to Patie (a simple marriage ceremony of holding hands, the union being dissoluble at the end of a year if there were no children) instead of properly wed (Act One, Scene Eight)? Or her disapproval of 'Coldstream' (unofficial or improper) marriages or by the way she scolds Liza for her frivolity, or giving Jenny and Liza a real tongue lashing for what they have been up to at the kirn? Do you think she is too critical or is just standing up for herself? Or is she possibly trying to protect the girls? Or has she forgotten what it is like to be young and is perhaps jealous of them?

She can also sometimes sound rather holier-than-thou in the way she gossips about others (for example, Act One, Scene Three or Scene Eight) though she is very honest in telling us that she made sure Andra was brought 'to account' (Act One, Scene Eight), how she had to shame him publicly and drag him into respectability by the scruff of the neck as he would not have entered into any kind of marriage relationship freely, as Patie and Sara did:

> MAGGIE: [...] You have to bring them to account. Andra wouldn't ask me. He *wouldn't*. He was never going to ask.

> So when he was standing with a crowd of lads, I flew to his
> neck and measured him for the sark. His wedding sark.

As already mentioned, she has some interesting similarities with another of Lewis Grassic Gibbon's heroines, Meg Menzies in his short story 'Smeddum', as Maggie leads her husband Andra to the altar, almost by the scruff of the neck, a bit like Meg does with some of her feckless family, though ironically she herself never married. Indeed, Meg has very different views on marriage.

Does her story make you feel admiration or sympathy for her as a young woman in a desperate situation (notice the italics at 'he wouldn't' and how she 'flew to his neck') or as a homemaker ensuring that fickle men show proper respect and act responsibly towards women and their children? Or does it reveal something unattractive about her?

She can also appear very disapproving and humourless, as in the way she finds nothing funny in the story about the lads swapping the babies after one of the kirns (Act Two, Scene Seven) and only sees the young men responsible in a very dim light, unlike Sara who appreciates their sense of humour and stands up for the boys.

However, as Liza's conflict with Maggie develops, the balance of sympathy probably starts to shift, though Glover is content simply to reveal her characters' strengths and weaknesses. In other words she allows them to speak for themselves and leaves us to make up our own minds about them. Throughout the play she lets us hear different viewpoints or opinions on people or events – for example, where we hear three different viewpoints on Steenie in Act One, Scene Seven.

As we have already seen, the kirn is the turning point in the play and we possibly start to feel more sympathy for Liza after this, mainly due to the fact that Maggie becomes increasingly critical of her, almost finding fault with her at every opportunity. In fact Maggie almost victimises Liza, calling her 'dirt' (Act Two, Scene Four) and refers to her as being 'just like her mother Maisie Kerr – no better than she should be. Tinkler trash!'. When Sara tells Maggie this is not fair, Maggie's reply is that 'you don't know the half of it [...] Flaunty piece of – dirtery!' and, later in the same scene, she calls her a 'sleekit piece of dirtery!'. This extremely vicious personal criticism may carry a degree of retaliation for Liza's earlier unkind remarks but it also clearly shows that she feels threatened by Liza, not simply because she seems to reject everything Maggie stands for, but perhaps also because she suspects, or even knows, that her husband Andra is lusting after the younger woman.

This in fact turns out to be true, though Liza only confesses it to Ellen later on as she obviously cannot tell Maggie. In contrast to Maggie's bitchiness at this stage of the play, Liza's confession reveals how miserable and how vulnerable she actually is, but even though she is upset by Andra's unwanted sexual attention, she surprisingly defends him from Ellen's ridicule because she values his kindness and admires his skill with animals. In spite of her own misery she is able to see him as a whole person and appreciate his strengths as well as his weaknesses, something that clearly sheds a new light on her character.

Perhaps Glover wants us to feel likewise for Maggie. While Liza's confession about Andra makes us feel sorry for her, it might also make us feel sympathy for Maggie at the same time, even though she seems much readier to blame the younger woman than her own husband. She might have a sharp tongue in her head, but if we judge her by her actions and not her words, you may feel that there is much to admire about her. Not only is she constantly multi-tasking and trying to make the best of things, but her down-to-earth common sense, honesty and 'smeddum' come to the fore several times.

Notice that even though Maggie is very angry with the girls when they return from the kirn, just before dawn, she also tries to stop them getting into trouble from the foreman and looks after Tottie to let Sara go to work, while she immediately takes charge of the situation when Kello falls and the others seem helpless. Above all she is outraged by what happened to Tottie and thinks Kello should have been brought to justice, while she also tries her best to convince Mr Elliott that Tottie is innocent and could not possibly have killed him. She appears genuinely upset by what happens to Tottie and attempts, without much success, to bring some comfort to Sara at the end, by trying to convince her that Tottie will be better off in the asylum. Perhaps this is cold comfort, but she is clearly trying to show kindness, though she mutters under her breath that it could have been a lot worse for Tottie (i.e. she could have been hanged).

Thus Glover helps us to see Maggie as well as Liza as rounded complex characters with strengths as well as weaknesses, leaving us to make up our own minds about them. Possibly Maggie's bark is often worse than her bite as she possesses a fierce, sometimes intolerant, sense of right and wrong, something perhaps very Scottish. At the same time there is something universal about this earthy, fertile and formidable matriarch who defends her brood ferociously, but sadly has little life of her own, sacrificing everything for her man and her family. Her whole identity is defined by her role as wife and mother.

Liza and Ellen
We first hear of Ellen in the conversation between Liza and Tottie in Act One, Scene Two and we immediately see that Tottie, who believes it was due to Ellen that they were hired, does not share Liza's critical view that Ellen 'never gave any favours'. Their conversation about her is used as an introduction to Ellen's monologue which is built round her answers to her own two questions – 'learn to use a fan?' and 'take tea with the gentry?' – which provide a series of contrasts between her new life of ease as Mistress Elliott and her previous hard life as a bondager. This is recalled via the long list of words describing the weather and the strenuous physical work, while her use of 'we' shows she still very much identifies with the bondagers, still considers herself one of them, all of which might make us disinclined to share Liza's critical view of her.

Yet even though Ellen is now dressed like a lady and she enumerates all the luxuries and privileges that astonish her (Act One, Scene Six), we also see that she is happy to see

her old friends Sara and Tottie and feels sympathy for the
women working out in the rain. In fact she is genuinely affectionate towards Tottie and we are told that Tottie's 'recipro-
cating hug is uninhibited, wholehearted'. Ellen also appears
to have no airs and graces about her while she is even able to
laugh at herself and her new situation. Even after Sara has
told Tottie that they must call her 'Mistress Elliott' now, they
both continue to call her by the old familiar diminutive 'Nell'
as if her new title does not quite fit her yet, while the idea
of assuming a new identity is conveyed via the symbolism of
her new dress and especially the stays that keep her upright
and will not let her bend. (See **Dramatic Technique and
Style: Dress and props**.)

Ironically Sara appears quite disapproving when Ellen
loosens her stays and lolls in the hay with Tottie as if she
enjoys being her old self again in the company of her friends.
Sara 'shakes her head at Nell's old ways' while Tottie calls
her 'bad Nell', though Ellen hastens to add 'not now! I'm a
married lady now!'. Tottie keeps referring to her as 'Ellen
Rippeth that was' as if she has become someone else, or is
someone playing a new role that she is not quite accustomed
to, but is enjoying nevertheless. When Sara sings the refrain
'And was she no very well off', she obviously means Ellen,
though as the play develops we discover that there is a price
to be paid for her new wealth and status.

When Liza first meets Ellen at the end of Act One, Scene
Six, the latter is lying in the hay but we see that she is 'not
put out at being caught lolling there by a servant' and is
not unfriendly as she asks Liza about her brother Steenie.
However, Liza's muttered comment, as Ellen exits, 'no thanks
to you if he's well', clearly reveals her bitterness towards her
new mistress. This helps to arouse our curiosity about the past
history between these two and we soon learn that Liza still
holds a grudge against Ellen for jilting her brother, Steenie.

Tottie's repeated muttering of 'Sas-katch-e-wan' at the end
of the above scene provides a bridge into the very short, but
very important Act One, Scene Seven, where Ellen, Sara and
Maggie speak from their 'separate areas' in a series of solilo-
quies that actually form a kind of dialogue, as each character

gives their opinion of Steenie and his reasons for running off to Canada. Sara's recollection of the beauty of that summer when 'they were a' mad for dancing' and Maggie's comment that Ellen 'drove them a' wild' help create the setting, mood and atmosphere for Ellen's longer dramatic monologue which ends the scene. This monologue would repay closer textual analysis to appreciate just how vivid, passionate and breathless her speech is, as she re-enacts the scene and answers her own questions 'why not?' and 'what did I get?'.

Notice especially how effectively Glover uses various linguistic devices like short dramatic sentences, incomplete or minor sentences, direct questions, exclamations, ellipsis, contrast, repetition, climactic structure and Ellen talking to herself at one point via the second person pronoun, perhaps suggesting that she now feels she was then someone else or that she now has to distance herself from that earlier Ellen, though her recollection is so fresh and so vivid.

Ellen's soliloquy reveals much about herself in a moment of very honest confession about how she seized the moment to 'set her cap at the maister'. Can we admire or criticise her for using her charms to 'better herself', as poor girls have done throughout history? Perhaps there is an element of truth in all the subjective viewpoints in this scene and Glover leaves us to make up our own mind about Steenie and Ellen, but Liza certainly has not forgiven her and a tension remains between them.

In contrast to Liza, Ellen appears to have 'got' what she wanted. But how far has she got what she really wanted, how far has she benefited from doing so? Though she is sympathetic to her old friends, she certainly relishes much about her new way of life and appreciates how fortunate she is to have escaped from bondage. And yet, as we see when she lolls in the hay or talks to Liza about the joys of working in the harvest, she clearly misses some things and perhaps there are deeper regrets and losses in her new life after all.

We also see her alternating between two different voices: firstly, speaking Scots as the former bondager with her old friends and, secondly, as Mistress Elliott who has to mix with gentry and learn how to 'speak posh' to address the visitors, as in Act Two, Scene Three. Here we see how far she has apparently changed as the mistress, now referring to the bondagers as 'they' and displaying a more detached attitude towards them, but, on the other hand, her soliloquy reveals her more ambivalent personal feelings both about the bondagers and the changes that have come over her, physically and emotionally. She recalls how Mister Elliott did not even know her name till she set her cap at him, but her confession, 'I'm all pale now [...] they've made a lady of me now', is very ambivalent. What do you think her reply 'almost' to Liza's question (Act Two, Scene Four) about loving 'the maister' reveals? How far do you think 'they've made a lady of me now' shows a sense of gain or loss, pride or regret or perhaps both?

Above all her new identity is not just a matter of dressing up and behaving like a lady. She is seen by her husband's mother as 'the new blood', a prize animal whose job is to produce 'prize sons' for the Elliotts and herein lies the cause of her desperation. By catching 'the maister, she got 'the Big Hoose', she 'got a' thing', but some things cannot be bought with money. In Act One, Scene Six when Tottie asks her if she is going to have a baby, she hesitates before replying 'not yet' and then confesses that 'the maister [...] keeps his passion under hidlings', i.e. hidden or covered up. However, Sara's kindly reassurance that 'there's time enough' is not what Ellen wants to hear by Act Two, Scene Six where she desperately seeks Sara's help to find a special herb to cure her barrenness and she openly confesses to how miserable she really is:

> ELLEN: [...] I need a child now! Not for me – well, not for me only – for the maister! [...] I'm useless in that great house! [...] He doesn't even know I've come into the room. He breaks my heart.

Ultimately, Ellen seems to be valued only as a means of providing sons, not valued for who she is, while her charms no longer seem to work on Mr Elliott as he is now too busy with other things. Clearly she has not 'got a' thing' and in ironic contrast to her being wealthy but barren, there is poverty and fecundity all around her: Maggie overburdened with bairns, the hinds who 'would have you swelled before they called the banns', and 'it happens soon enough for those that don't want it, who don't even think about it'.

Just as Elliott did not know Ellen's name at first, he is always just 'the maister' or 'Maister Elliott' and he is never even given a first name, though in those days it was common for wives to address their husbands as 'Mister' and she would always have referred to him as 'the maister' in front of others. At the end of the play there are no 'prize sons' and the Elliotts have lost their lease, in spite of generations of them working Blacksheils, so for Ellen life is once again precarious and the future uncertain. Perhaps she would have been happier with Steenie after all?

However, just as things change profoundly for both Liza and Ellen during the course of the play, so does their relationship, something that is central to our understanding of both characters. In spite of Liza's resentment, Ellen's honesty and openness gradually help Liza to form a bond with her, rooted in their experience of working the land and expressed in their shared description of the earthy nature of women's work in Act One, Scene Ten. This leads them on to contrast all the earthy work with the beauty of harvest time, thereby revealing that both are sensitive to the joy of the ripening corn and bringing in the harvest, which 'whispers' to Liza like a person and arouses in Ellen a very sensual and almost erotic pleasure – 'I gloried in the shearing' – giving her an almost supernatural strength like an Amazon, or a Corn Queen, a pagan goddess of fertility who would cut down Mabon (lord of the harvest, or divine son of the Mother Earth goddess in pagan mythology) if he stood in her way. Ironically she is not fertile, but at the end of this scene they smile at each other, indicating a very significant improvement in their relationship.

We can also see how far Liza has changed in her attitude to Ellen by looking at Act Two, Scene Four where Ellen offers her sympathy and support after Maggie's harsh criticism. Liza then shows her trust by confessing to Ellen about Andra, something which Ellen cannot help laughing at,

though not at Liza's expense, and she goes on to reassure her
that she knows Liza is not 'a bad girl' as she herself once was.
Confronted with Ellen's honesty about herself and Steenie,
we see that, although Liza still thinks he ran off to Canada
because of Ellen, she does not now feel any bitterness against
her, only sadness for the loss of her brother. In defence of her
treatment of Steenie, Ellen describes Liza and her brother
as 'two of a kind [...] fresh pats of butter still waiting for
the stamp', (i.e. the stamp pressed into the butter with the
maker's name) meaning they are both young and innocent,
though we are clearly aware that the stamp of life and experience is now firmly pressing down on Liza.

Liza and Steenie
We have already discussed Liza's resentment towards Ellen
regarding Steenie's emigration. His letter from Canada is
also a major turning point in Liza's life and a moment of
revelation in the play. The arrival of such a letter would have
been a very rare event, the cause of great excitement, and
Glover uses it to create a moment of real drama, almost like
a play within a play, firstly with Liza fiercely fighting Tottie
and then cajoling her to get the letter back and everyone
gathering round to listen to Liza reading it out and sharing
her letter as if it concerns them all. Liza is both thrilled and
apprehensive at receiving a letter from Steenie about his new
life in Canada, but much to her disappointment it contains
little or nothing of a personal nature.

When she comes to the last paragraph and he refers to his
'wife', she stops dead and we see not only how surprised but
also how deeply hurt she is at the sudden realisation that now
he has a wife, he 'belongs to her less' and won't be needing her
in Canada. Notice also the cruel parallel with Sara's situation
as she will never receive a letter, even if Patie could write. As
the other girls dance a jig and sing 'Woo'd and Married' in a
kind of belated long-distance wedding celebration, Liza does
not join in and she drifts off to a quiet corner still holding the
letter, tracing the seal and the writing with her finger as if
trying to communicate with Steenie by touching what he has
touched, a very moving symbol of love, separation and loss.

Liza and Kello

As we have seen when discussing the plot, Glover builds up certain expectations that are not fulfilled as we may anticipate that Liza's attraction to Kello will develop into the main strand in the drama. While this does not work out as expected, it is still a very important element and we are clearly shown the effect of Kello's behaviour on Liza as well as others. In Act One, Scene Four we hear her expressing her admiration for his dancing ability and when she and Jenny try the Halloween ritual she dances about with excitement and only has to nod her head to admit that she saw Kello in the glass, meaning she wants him as her 'dearie'.

She is also linked to Kello in dance and in song as she inserts his name in the last two lines of 'O, the plooman's so bonny' when she is dancing at the start of the kirn scene. In spite of her avowal not to wed when Tottie blurts out, just before the kirn, that she saw her with Kello in the turnip house, Liza's defence that he was only showing her the dance steps does not sound too convincing, especially as she now tries to be very friendly to Tottie for a change. It would also appear that Liza and Jenny were thinking about running off to Coldstream Brig for a bit of fun (possibly signifying an informal betrothal) though they either changed their minds or their lads, Kello and Dave, were too drunk. When Tottie returns home in the dawn from the kirn, Liza at first refuses to believe her story, but by the end of the scene she tells Jenny he's 'not mine' and she'll 'spit' if he tries to speak to her.

Even after she knows what Kello did, the way she describes his grace and agility on horseback shows that she is clearly still infatuated by this black-eyed 'Gyptian' charmer who 'dances so trig [...] stroked my hair'. It takes Ellen's blunt truth about his promiscuous behaviour to snap her out of her dream and resort to a face-saving lie to conceal her hurt, pretending that she knows all about him when clearly she does not. Yet in the dramatic climax of the play, her howls open the scene as she screams for help and her confused, broken and repetitive short statements ('It's Kello. It's Kello [...] There's no one there') betray the depth of her pain and despair. In her last line in this scene (her second last in the whole play) she is obviously trying to defend herself from any criticism from Maggie, by stressing that she was not going to the stables, i.e. to see Kello, but going to the dairy. Whether we find this believable or not, we are now watching a very changed Liza from the one we saw at the start.

Thus we see Liza suffering several painful disappointments or losses in the play and by the end probably view her much more sympathetically than we did at the start. After Kello's accident, Sara tries to soothe her and ironically sits her down by the cradle to look after the baby while Maggie goes for help. This is the first time in the whole play that we see Liza looking after the baby (who now has a name for the first time – Wee Joe) and, though her mind is clearly on other matters, placing her at the cradle perhaps implies that one day this will inevitably be her role too, in contrast to the rebellious and independent young woman we first met at the hiring fair.

Liza and Sara

Liza only speaks once more in the play but it is the very last line, thus making her words linger in our memory and also creating a huge contrast to her opening lines. It is also a superb example of how a few simple words can be easily overlooked. They may not sound important, but when placed in the context of the whole drama they actually speak volumes. Liza now turns to Sara for help, hoping that they will perhaps move to the same farm, though in the way she hesitates and gently repeats Sara's name, we can see that she is now able to sympathise with the plight of the older woman and realise that Sara too is in need of friendship and support after Tottie has been taken away. Her last sentence is a very simple question to Sara, but, bearing in mind her resistance to the idea of learning how to spin earlier in the play, it highlights how far she has travelled as a person and implies a great deal more about her than simply wanting to learn a new skill. The young woman is now bonding with the older woman and ready to learn from her, rather like an orphan adopting a mother, a mother who has just had her own child taken from her.

LIZA: Sara? ... We'll maybe get to the same farm, Sara. If
we do – will you teach me to spin?

Throughout the play, Sara acts as a substitute mother
figure to the other women, exerting a wise and kindly influence and always acting as tactful peacemaker, especially
between Liza and Maggie, as in Act One, Scenes Nine and
Eleven. (Perhaps in calling her Sara, Glover is making an
allusion to the biblical matriarch, Sarah, wife of Abraham,
famous for her beauty, wisdom and the gift of prophecy?)
Her tolerant views on love and marriage, rooted in an older
Scotland (for example, her use of the custom of hand-fasting),
are contrasted with Maggie's strictly conventional Victorian
values in Act One, Scene Eight where we hear Sara's loving
description of her partner Patie and why she could not step
onto the boat at Greenock to emigrate with him. She is pain-
fully torn between love of her homeland and her love for a
man whom she loses as a consequence of her decision, but
she hopes he is now happily married with bairns, as 'he was
made for happiness'. However, she does not in any way feel
resentful about anything or feel burdened by Tottie, but feels
blessed for having her. We also see her warm sense of humour
and folk wisdom in her stories about the lads swopping the
babies around after the kirn or in her own mother's little
parable about trying to steal some of her neighbour's corn.
We are not told her exact age, but she cannot be particularly old as Tottie is still only fifteen. While a bondager would
have aged very quickly, Glover clearly makes her seem much
older than she actually would be, so that we think of her as
someone deeply rooted in her place, her 'calf-ground', as if
she is part of the land itself, knowing every nook and crannie
of it, like the place where a special plant once grew to help
women become fertile. In many ways she is a traditional
wise woman or 'skeely wife', a healer to whom the others all
turn for help or advice of one kind or another, as Ellen does
when she is unable to produce a child. Sara's advice is both
sympathetic and sensible: no magic plant grows there now to
help Ellen but instead she must be patient and find love and
happiness in her relationship with 'the maister'.

Though Sara always wishes happiness for others, she finds little for herself after the child she loves, and protects, is 'stolen' from her by Kello's drunken sexual exploitation, turning the friendly and innocent Tottie into a disturbed and distraught adolescent who is eventually blamed for Kello's death. Yet in spite of all this she can even feel pity for Kello and can articulate the real tragedy of his untimely death:

> SARA: Poor Kello. He was daft himself [...] And yet ... no heart ... no thought ... no soul. That's what was wrong [...] Poor young Kello. He was the one who wasn't all there. (Act Two, Scene Nine)

She means that, although he had many attractive qualities, he lacked the essential imaginative ability of being able to feel for others, to put himself in their place and care about the consequences of his own actions on others. Thus unlike Sara, he 'wasn't all there' as a fully developed, mature human being.

Tottie's capture and incarceration are extremely painful for her mother but though Sara is grief-stricken at the end, she is still able to show concern for Ellen and presumably Liza. It is also very significant that Glover gives Sara the final long speech in the play, repeating Tottie's stories about the ghost in 'the lang syne rigs' and his bleak vision of a future without folk. Sara is therefore an extremely important figure in the play: the tribal wise woman and healer of wounds, both physical and psychological, possessing an emotional intelligence and sympathy for other human beings. She also possesses the imaginative insight to understand and appreciate the significance of Tottie's visions.

Tottie

While Liza possesses some of the qualities of a conventional central character who undergoes important changes during the drama, Tottie sneaks under the radar to replace her as the main focus in Act Two, as events take a very surprising turn. Indeed it is Tottie's cruel victimisation, as well as the hurt and disappointment suffered by the others that creates such a powerful conclusion and pushes the play close to a tragic ending.

While all the other women are given common Scottish names of the period, her childlike name stands out as being different, just as she herself is different from others. The name Tottie, (or totie, a small person, tot or toddler) fits her very well as she really is still a child in many ways, but 'tottie' is also a variant of 'tattie' (potato) a term that was used contemptuously for a simpleton, someone with a soft or empty head. Yet her mother does not treat her as someone stupid, but protects her as a very 'special' child who has needs and qualities other 'normal' people do not.

At the start of the play, she appears as a friendly but 'slow' child who sometimes still wants to play, though the other children mock her as 'a daftie'. Likewise none of the other girls, especially Liza, want much to do with her at first and they mock her childlike attempts to join in their Halloween ritual. However, when Liza offers to teach her the steps of the dances for the kirn, Tottie declines and instead performs her own wild dance which 'kills Liza's waltz' (see **Dramatic Technique and Style: Movement, dance and mime**). At this point she becomes the centre of attention, thereby fore-shadowing what will happen, as ironically it is Tottie, not Liza that gets Kello at the kirn.

While everyone treats her as simple, she sees and hears things the others do not (such as knowing what Jenny and Liza have been doing, or her meeting with the 'ghost' in the 'lang syne rigs') and she believes she saw Kello in the glass at Halloween, thus ironically predicting her fate. Like Liza, she too is fascinated by 'the Gyptian' and when she eventually reappears the morning after the kirn, she displays a childish glee in having beaten Liza to win the prize. However, once the disbelief and shock of the others have subsided, the full impact of her sexual exploitation is apparent in the way she naively believes that a drunken ploughman's rough sexual fumbling means she is going to be married and in the defiant way she tells her mother she isn't 'the bairnie now'. The ugly reality of what Kello has done is fully conveyed through violent or sordid expressions like 'pushed me agin the stack' and 'smoor the fleas together' while she confesses 'it hurt' and there is blood on her skirt. She is indeed 'hurt' but it is much more than a physical hurt and the full extent of how badly she is hurt soon becomes apparent in Act Two.

As Sara says, Kello 'stole' Tottie from her, but he has not just stolen her virginity, he has also stolen the innocent, happy child she once was, 'changed' her into a confused and disturbed adolescent who becomes almost a stranger to her mother and grows increasingly angry and aggressive, beating her own body against a haystack and brandishing her graip violently like a weapon. Whereas earlier in the play we saw how she was soothed by rocking the cradle and telling her 'ghost' story to the baby, she now pushes the cradle with her hoe and leaves it rocking, something that arouses fear in Maggie.

However, in Act Two she again 'confides' to the baby, telling him the truth about what happened to Kello, and, because she has nothing to hide and is not capable of telling lies, we know that this is indeed the truth. Perhaps she can tell Maggie's baby her deepest secrets because she has more in common with the child than with the adults around her who do not understand her and would only dismiss her words as those of a 'daftie'. Ironically only a child hears the truth, things that adults cannot be told, do not want to hear or would not believe anyway.

At the end of the play Tottie's capture and removal to the asylum are extremely cruel and painful to watch. We fully understand, unlike 'the maister', that a completely innocent, sexually exploited child has been blamed for the death of her exploiter and that, because of her disturbing behaviour, she must be locked away by her society as a dangerous lunatic. The travesty of justice is skilfully conveyed in Act Two, Scene Nine where Maggie tries hard to tell 'the maister' that Bella Monteith is lying and that it could not have been Tottie that killed Kello. We never see Mister Elliott or hear him speak, but his questions and even their tone are cleverly implied in the way Maggie struggles to justify her answers, and especially in the way she is finally cut short and dismissed when she tries to speak the truth about Tottie. He clearly finds it easier and safer to believe Bella's story, especially as Tottie has been running after Kello and behaving strangely.

Glover therefore emphasises how Tottie suffers for things others have done to her and is victimised through the evils and failures of 'normal' adults. Although Maggie tries hard to console Sara at the end, she is right in calling Tottie 'a poor maimed creature' while her mother clearly feels that her incarceration is really a kind of death, the death of an innocent yet strangely wise child. If you have read *Of Mice and Men* by John Steinbeck, you might see several similarities but also important differences between Lennie and Tottie.

Thus Glover gives Tottie a very important and central role in the play: someone who is regarded as 'not all there' is given intuitive powers of seeing and knowing things 'normal' people simply do not know, as if possessed of a kind of sixth sense or 'second sight', someone who can tune into the presence of people from the past and even glimpse the future, a bit like a traditional 'seer'. Although her father Patie knew 'she wasn't quite natural', she is very natural in another sense. We learn from the children's cruel jeering how she was conceived in the corn rigs and so she is a child of nature, born of a very natural loving relationship. Just as her mother is rooted in her 'calf ground', Tottie is closely attached to the place that produced her and in tune with its 'ghosts' from its past.

Thus she can sense the presence of the ancient 'plooman' in 'the lang syne rigs' up on the moor, can actually smell his oxen and 'feel the beasts on the ground' through her feet as if the past is still alive in the present. Thus she sees the vision of the man 'twixt me and the sun' who tells of a future world of plenty dominated by machinery that will not need horses or folk so that she is already a ghost like him, a thing of the past who will haunt 'fields without folk'. We only hear Tottie telling the baby or talking to herself about this but her mother recalls her strange story at the very end of the play, thereby stressing its importance as a central theme of the work.

THE MEN

Although the men all play an important role in the drama, they never actually appear, as if they are not quite all there in more ways than one, but their 'presence' is still powerful and their influence unavoidable in the lives of the women. Why do you think Glover has chosen to leave all her male characters offstage?

Kello

Kello, the black-eyed swarthy ploughman, looks at first as if he might become the focus of the heroine's romantic interest in the play for he possesses an almost devilish charm that makes him irresistible to some women. He can charm horses and women and probably thinks his good looks and charms will always get him what he wants. He is a great dancer and possesses incredible horseback tumbling skills, so it is rather ironic that he is killed as a result of a tumble where he is not able to perform somersaults and land on his feet when falling from the hay loft. Do you see this perhaps as a kind of ironic rough justice or retribution, reminding us of the biblical warning 'as ye sow so shall ye reap'? Is he a sort of devil in disguise who gets what he deserves or do you share Sara's more sympathetic feelings about him? (See also the discussion on **Liza and Kello** above.)

The maister, Mr Elliott

The men all appear immature, selfish or lacking in some way. Mr Elliott, 'the maister', is regarded as strict but fair, in many ways the ideal master, who perhaps represents a traditional sort of Scottish male authority. He is clearly enterprising and innovative and runs the 'model farm' that attracts visitors from overseas, but he has no sons to pass this on to. He may have been seduced into marriage by Ellen's charms, but he is obviously now too focused on his work and career to have sufficient time for any love or affection, leaving Ellen unfulfilled and unhappy. It is also rather ironic that he is fighting to win better wages and conditions for farm workers, but he himself is victimised for his political views by the Earl who refuses to renew his lease on a farm his family have worked for generations to improve. Thus at the end he too has no security, although we learn that his future might lie in politics as he is planning to stand for Parliament. Yet in spite of his campaign on behalf of others, he presides over a real travesty of justice by failing to discover the truth about Kello's death, probably because it is more convenient to simply blame 'the daftie'.

Andra

Andra, the hind, represents the poorest agricultural farm labourer of the period who has no security of tenure what-soever and, like the bondagers he has to hire, spends a life moving from farm to farm, but unlike the maister he has a very large family indeed, though this does not seem to stop him lusting after young bondagers. We are given three different perspectives on him by the women: his wife Maggie, Liza and Ellen. Although Maggie appears proud of him and is very defensive of him, he obviously had to be forced into marriage by her, probably because he was reluctant to face up to his responsibilities, perhaps like Kello. He clearly lied to Liza about the number of children he has and he lusts after her, something Ellen finds laughable as she obviously sees him as 'a tumshie', (a turnip, i.e. not very handsome or very bright) though ironically Liza stands up for him because she can appreciate his better qualities, particularly his skill and gentleness with animals, something that is perhaps lacking in his dealings with women, again like Kello.

The other men

While the other lads on the farm dispense their own kind of rough justice on Kello for what he did to Tottie, by 'douking' him in the trough and kicking him round the yard, they soon start to feel sorry for him, while some even admire him and blame Tottie instead, as if she somehow deserved it. The maister would also find it much more convenient to put the blame on the 'daftie' as he would not want to lose a skilful horseman.

Although Sara recalls how loving and kind Patie was, he still put his desire to find a new life in Canada before his wife

and daughter, while Steenie, slighted in love by Ellen, could
even be accused of leaving his sister to run off to Canada
and, like Patie, putting his own ambitions first. They both
represent the wandering or ambitious Scot who has fled his
native land and its poverty to find success and prosperity
in the 'new world'. Steenie's letter from Canada, already
discussed, highlights some very striking contrasts between
the two countries as well as possibly providing an alternative
perspective on our relationship with the land. (See **Further
Discussion of Themes**, p. 48.)

Although the men are shown with some good or attractive qualities, they are definitely 'not all there' in one way or
another, as a very essential human quality is indeed missing.
Is this an accurate or fair representation, or an over-critical
or stereotypical picture of men by a feminist author?

5. DRAMATIC TECHNIQUE AND STYLE

In a number of ways, *Bondagers* is a very realistic and convincing depiction of nineteenth-century rural life. In order to create a highly authentic sense of time and place, to make us see what it looked like, sounded like, even smelt like, Glover dresses the women in the actual type of clothing worn by bondagers, paying a great deal of attention to details, such as the protective rags wrapped round their hands and straw rope leggings. She also deploys many of the farm implements they would have used as they work or talk about work, while at a linguistic level her characters speak just enough Scots, including a few archaisms, to capture something of the voice of these long-vanished field workers. All of this helps to sustain the illusion of reality, that we are actually hearing and seeing nineteenth-century farm workers going about their working lives.

Set and staging

At the same time, especially in terms of its dramatic style and staging, the play is very eclectic as Glover also uses many elements of non-naturalistic drama, verse drama and expressionist theatre. In order to create maximum freedom of space and facilitate easy movement from indoors to outdoors, and in fact to emphasise the links between the two, Glover dispenses with any scenery and keeps stage furniture or properties to a minimum, thereby deliberately avoiding anything that would 'fix' or limit the action to any one 'realistic' location. In addition, she deploys light and sound, mime, movement, dance, song, rhyme and monologue to great effect in order to suggest locations, create mood, weather, time of year and, more importantly, to reveal character and convey her themes to the audience. All of this gives her a great deal of spatial freedom and imaginative scope to switch scenes simply and quickly and let the drama flow across space and time without any physical hindrance whatsoever. Glover in fact comments on this in her introduction: 'all areas "come and go", as it were'.

Thus the action moves easily from one location to another or more than one location is used simultaneously, as in Act One, Scene Seven, where the characters speak from their 'separate areas' to let the audience see Steenie from different perspectives. We also see Maggie or Tottie still minding the baby in one area of the stage while others are working else-where, in the fields or in the stables, or we see Ellen in Act Two, Scene Three switching between addressing the visitors in her posh voice and speaking to herself in her own private area of the stage.

Sound and lighting

Staging is also effectively supported by changes in lighting or the use of sound effects to suggest different times of the year, day or place, for example summer and winter scenes or working in the fields in contrast to working indoors during wet weather. Bright clear lighting in Act One, Scene Four would help to suggest oppressive heat and sweaty labour in the fields, with the voices shouting from the far end of the field conveying a sense of distance and wide open spaces. In contrast, the dark scenes of early morning at the end of Act One or the cold winter scenes at the beginning of Act Two use very dim lighting and deploy harsh rattling or drumming offstage to help suggest a dark, cold world outside where sounds ring out across a frozen landscape with the ground as hard as iron. The action also moves very quickly from a night time scene to daytime or vice versa, for example the girls' fun in the dark with the mirror and candle in the short Halloween ritual in Act One, Scene Ten which falls between much longer outdoor working scenes, thereby helping to suggest the brevity of the night in contrast to the length of the working day.

Dress and props

Glover stresses how distinctive and unique the bondagers' dress was, describing it as 'almost a uniform' (as depicted in the painting *Berwickshire Field-workers* by Edward Arthur Walton, 1884). While it does not need to be totally authen-tic, 'something approximating it is essential' to capture this distinctiveness. She suggests boots or clogs (though in summer they sometimes worked in their bare feet which would have been as tough as leather) full skirts with two or three petticoats, 'headhankies' i.e. 'kerchiefs that covered their heads [...] But the bondagers' most notable trade-mark, worn over the headhankie, was a black straw bonnet: trimmed with red ruching and lined with the same sprigged cotton that they used for their blouses. Muddy, sometimes shabby, but beguiling'. (Glover's introduction)

The removal or addition of clothing emphasises their constant battle with the elements, especially at the height of summer and the depth of winter, just as the songs, rhymes and chants express their bond to the land and the cycle of the seasons. In Act One, Scene Four, when they are bent singling turnips, they are not 'individually recognisable' due to their large hats and headhankies worn to protect them from the sun. An older woman, probably Sara, warns a younger one, probably Liza, to bind more rags or straw round her hands to protect them and at the start of the next scene we see Liza slumped and tired, unwinding these rags from her hands, so that we can almost feel the cuts and blisters.

In contrast, at the start of Act Two, we see Tottie dressed like a right 'tumshie bogle' (scarecrow) 'swathed for winter (as are the rest of the cast, but not quite so wildly) – straw rope leggings, her arm covered in extra knitted oversleeves; fingerless mitts, shawl, the headhankie pulled protectively well around the face'. Yet in spite of all their layers of protec-tive clothing, the rhymes and choral lines help us to feel the bitter cold of early January so effectively that perhaps we can also feel them shivering under all these layers.

We are also given a clear picture of the physically demand-ing nature of their work in the way they wear coarse sacking aprons and 'breech their claes' or 'kirtle up' their skirts, so that they are almost like trousers by pulling their skirts from behind up between their legs, and pinning them at the front to make a kind of divided skirt. In Act One, Scene Ten this visual picture complements the language and imagery used by Liza and Ellen to describe the filthy nature of their work and how at the end of the day, especially after turning over a dunghill 'higher than your head, wider than a house', both clothes and skin were stinking. 'Woman's work', Ellen says sarcastically, when the way they are dressed and the long list of short sentences beginning with verbs related to work, along with the repetition of various words for dung, all help to convey a sense of their tough muscularity, even masculinity and the very earthy nature of a bondager's never-ending toil to make the land fertile.

Clothing is also used to emphasise the huge gulf that exists between the social levels of bondager and farmer's wife. When we first see Ellen in Act One, Scene Six, the contrast between her new way of life and her former is immediately highlighted through the huge difference in clothing and physical condition between her and the field workers, for example the bondagers being 'drookit', Sara suffering from rheumatism and Ellen's 'shoothers always dry now', though if she does get wet she now has someone to fetch dry shoes and stockings for her. Unlike the bondagers, who are doing wet weather work in coarse working clothes, Ellen appears in the fine new gown she wears for taking tea with other farmers' wives and we see her adjusting and admiring her clothes as if she cannot quite believe her own good luck in now being 'Mistress Elliott'. Sara warns Tottie to 'mind' Ellen's gown, but we soon start to see how uncomfortable Ellen actually is in her new role as she has to sit down very carefully 'like a lady' who 'can't bend forrard, can't bend back' because of her stays. She is now 'tied up every morning – let loose at bedtime' rather like a prize animal and when Ellen gets Tottie to loosen her stays, she 'lolls in the hay, more like the bondager she used to be', as if she is enjoying her temporary release from the unnatural behaviour, manners and restrictions she now has to endure as the price of being a lady instead of a bondager. Ironically it is perhaps a new kind of bondage in some ways. (See **Characters and Themes: Liza and Ellen**.)

While Glover does not use any stage sets or furniture, she is very specific about some of the stage properties, mainly farming implements and the tools of their work: the hoes, graips and sickles, the latter used to symbolise the ancient nature of their work and bond to the land. When not working in the fields, we see them working indoors, as in Act One, Scene Six where they are 'busy cleaning horse tack or patching and sewing sacks, or winding the home-made straw rope into neat oval balls', so that the stage is sometimes cluttered with various bits of equipment or 'gear' required for work they are rarely allowed to put down. All of these are easily carried on and off and do not interfere with the fluidity of action but they add considerably to the sense of authenticity as well as the theme of the drama.

One important prop rarely, if ever, leaves the stage – the cradle – which Glover says in her introduction, 'is a state-ment and should be visible'. The cradle holds Maggie's baby and is a constant visible reminder of a woman's traditional role as bearer of children and mother, a role that Maggie defends vigorously against Liza's criticisms. It is cruelly ironic that Maggie is overburdened with children, but Ellen, who is regarded as 'the new blood' by her husband's mother, is desperate for a child but cannot produce one. At different times both Maggie and Tottie are comforted or calmed by rocking the cradle or by picking the baby up or talking to it. Unlike Liza, Tottie is fascinated by babies and her mono-logues to Maggie's baby are extremely important, revealing her strange visions about the ghost of the ancient farmer or about what really happened to Kello when he fell from the hay loft. (See also **Characters and Themes: Tottie.**)

Movement, dance and mime

Movement and mime are extremely important in this play both in terms of providing a very powerful visual represen-tation and celebration of the bondagers' physical work and at the same time operating symbolically as an important thematic device. We can see this in the opening scene where movement supports voice to suggest the hustle and bustle of the crowd or near the end of Act One in the way they all act out the kirn dances. In a play about farm workers Glover clearly needs to let us see her women working and even feel what that must have been like: toiling in the fields in all weathers, preparing for work or talking about work in one way or another, usually in a group, planting, hoeing, weeding or turning hay, as in Act One, Scene Four where they are bending down to single (i.e. thin out) turnips.

In this scene they never stop working and the dialogue 'when it comes, is fast, fragmented and overlapping', while we are also told 'they work fast, each moving along her own drill, keeping more or less in pace with the others'. All of this conveys the physical effort of their backbreaking work and even at times their breathlessness, through the pauses and gaps in the dialogue, so that we almost feel their need to 'flex their backs' towards the end of the scene. In Act One, Scene Ten, Ellen recalls how she could not straighten her back after 'howking tatties':

> ELLEN: At the end of the day I used to scraffle on all fours.
> I couldn't get to my feet till I was half way down the loan.

Even when they are not working outside or their work is over for the day, they are often seen mending, cleaning or tending to something and, in fact, Sara seems to feel guilty if they are not working, especially when Ellen is around, in case they are thought to be lazy workers exploiting their friendship with her. From the very first moment we see Maggie, she is constantly on the move, trying to do several things at once, showing us visually and emotionally the multi-tasking, never-ending work of a cottar's wife with eight bairns living in very cramped conditions with no rest or security. No wonder she laughs scornfully at Ellen's dream of lying in bed feeding a baby in the morning.

In the field scenes, we see the women all dressed the same, working in unison as part of a team who are highly dependent on each other and this is expressed via repetitive and rhythmic, almost ritualistic, movements, to convey the rhythms of their physically exhausting work in the fields from which a strange bond with the land and nature emerges, especially at harvest time. Thus we are shown human toil and fertility in tune with the rhythm and cycle of the seasons, conveying a clear sense of the human strengths and bonds the women share, while also bringing to life a shared culture, something highlighted in their communal celebrations via song, dance, ancient pagan rituals and superstitions which are shown to be far more powerful in their lives than anything the kirk can offer.

Thus a powerful sense of ritual and rhythm is expressed visually via movement and supported by songs and dances. Earlier in the play Sara recalls how one particular summer they were all 'mad for dancing – danced every night till the first field was cut' and on the night of the kirn there was 'a real harvest moon' when Ellen had her way with 'the maister'. This 'madness' is conveyed very dramatically during the kirn scene in Act One as everyone is affected by the collective excitement and sexual energy of the harvest home, especially the younger girls indulging in old fertility rituals, singing and practising their dance steps.

Yet it is surely highly significant that Glover increasingly puts Tottie centre stage in this scene, firstly by having her tell about what Jenny and Liza have been up to with the saddler and the 'Gyptian', then refusing to dance Liza's waltz, even mocking Liza in her own version of the 'plooman' song and finally performing her own rough, highly spirited, clog or boot dance which 'kills Liza's waltz'. Possibly this suggests that Tottie's instinctive, primitive dance is much more powerful, more in tune with the spirit of the kirn and of the land itself, than this new fashionable elegant foreign dance, the waltz.

Everyone then joins in Tottie's song and dance, repeating the lines, but singing different lines to each line of the tune, adding to the raucous uncontrollable energy of it all, as if they are all part of it but doing their own thing and at the same time beating out the rhythm on the ground with farm implements to create a wild frenzied climax, thereby expressing their bond with each other and with mother earth. This dance in fact 'becomes the kirn' before coming to an abrupt halt, leaving the rest of the kirn to be enacted offstage via the interplay between Tottie listing the repertoire of dances and the others delivering a rhythmic chorus of calls and toasts. Thus at the height of the kirn, Glover lets us feel the wild primitive energy of the harvest celebrations mainly through Tottie's dance which lingers in the mind and in some ways also helps prepare us for the very unexpected outcome of Act One.

In contrast to Tottie's dance in this scene, her anger, hurt and isolation are expressed by very different actions or forms of movement in Act Two, Scene Two, such as brandishing a graip, possibly with tin cans attached to it, beating the ground, throwing herself against a stack, lashing out, killing the mowdies and repeating the ploughman song in a very different tone.

Glover also makes clever use of various vocal devices, choruses, songs and rhymes to create crowd scenes, communal events or celebrations, like Halloween or Hogmanay. In a play with a small cast, these devices not only allow her to 'rent a crowd' as it were, so that we almost forget there are only six characters in her play, but also help to place the individual characters in their wider social context and link her six women to a whole way of life which depends on an army of bondagers and farm labourers.

In the opening scene at the hiring fair, before we hear any individual character voices, we hear a series of anonymous solo voices, with words, phrases or comments repeated or overlapping, almost like a Greek chorus, beginning with the repetition of 'The Hiring [...] Hiring Fair', followed by a series of exclamations, familiar greetings and questions about people and places and ending with a list of farm names. At the same time a gradual increase in both pace of delivery and volume are used along with movement (for example, Liza being jostled) to create the noise, bustle and excitement of a crowd and, as the scene progresses, we hear a chorus repeating key lines and phrases to set the scene or to provide essential information about their work and payments. All of this helps establish a sense of community and shared experience, as well as convey-ing some of the cultural conventions or codes which frame the individual bondager's hopes, fears and expectations that we gradually start to hear about from the characters.

Songs and rhymes

Traditional songs and rhymes are vital ingredients in *Bondagers* as they perform a key role in creating a sense of community, reflecting characters' emotions and changing the mood of the play but also perhaps in providing a sort of indirect comment on events. Examples of these songs are 'Woo'd and Married an a', 'For the Sake o Somebody', 'Up in the Mornin' (the last two are regarded as Burns songs) plus 'O the Plooman's so Bonny', a song Glover actually made up to an old tune but it does sound like an authentic traditional song which Liza obviously adapts to suit her own situation.

Consider where each is used, what sort of mood is created by it and also how the theme of each song relates to the action and theme of the play. Look closely at how two very different moods are created at the beginning and end of the kirn scene (Act One, Scene Twelve) through the use of song, especially how the mood is subtly altered by the use of the song 'Somebody' at the end.

Also examine how the same song (such as 'Woo'd and Married', 'O the Plooman's so Bonny' and the Hogmanay chant) used in a different context later in the play or repeated by someone, especially Tottie, can create quite a different mood. At least two of the songs also turn out to be rather ironic. Is the ploughman really 'so bonnie and the best o them a' and is the wife really 'very well off'?

Bairn rhymes, chants and taunts are also a very significant feature of the play. Glover suggests the option of using offstage voices or the cast onstage acting as children which might have the advantage of implying a hidden, childish, cruel streak in the adults' attitude towards Tottie. We first hear them in Act One, Scene Five after Tottie has told the baby about the ghost and the children are heard taunting her in a 'loud, matter-of-fact unkind' manner, reminding us not only how cruel children can be but also repeating things they must have heard from adults, especially their jeering chant about how her mother 'lay with Wabster' and 'gat ye in the cornrigs'.

At Hogmanay the children's rhyme 'We're only some bits o bairns come oot to play' might seem innocent enough, but the children's voices are for the most part far from innocent, as they become increasingly cruel and hurtful, especially in the second last scene of the play when Tottie is very disturbed and about to be taken away. Tottie's repetition of the children's verses is very different in mood and tone, as it becomes increasingly dark, disturbed and violent, possibly suggesting that this adult 'child' is now very damaged and no one, apart from her mother, really cares. Thus songs and verses help to express the damage and the evil done to her by irresponsible, thoughtless, unfeeling men, the ones who are really 'not all there'.

Nearly all the songs and rhymes revolve around Halloween, the kirn and Hogmanay, the associated customs and rituals of which all contribute a great deal to the play. Not only do they help create mood and atmosphere, but they also help to emphasise important stages in the plot while at the same time enhancing the themes of the play. These ancient rural customs with pagan origins were still a living part of a communal culture before the age of the mass media and they help create a sense of community and closeness, the pleasure and pain the women all share as well as their never-ending work. They also provide strong links to the past and help convey a sense of continuity and communion with ancestors and ancient times, a bit like Tottie's visions and ghosts. The Halloween customs in particular recall Burns' poem 'Halloween' which also describes the superstition acted out by the girls with the glass and the apple to foretell their future partners. This of course plays a crucial part in the plot but it does not turn out the way Liza hoped it would.

Further investigation and discussion points
Study other crowd scenes, especially the kirn, Act One, Scene Twelve or the Hogmanay and winter scenes at the start of Act Two. Try to identify how the interplay of movement, anonymous and individual voices, especially the listing and repetition of names, places or dances, and the use of songs help to set the scene and evoke atmosphere. Or examine the different techniques Glover uses to convey the never-ending, filthy nature of their work in Act One, Scene Ten, especially the repetition of the different words for dung!

Notice how at the start of Act Two we hear a solo voice singing 'Up in the Morning's no for me' and then other voices join in a 'spoken round' which not only adds to the volume but suggests the whole community is speaking here. As the chorus fades out, they repeat 'winter ... winter ... winter' before we hear the sudden burst of noise from the children, rattling, drumming and calling out the Hogmanay verse. This fades out and we again hear an anonymous series of short repetitive phrases describing the winter, spoken singly in turn, in a 'whispery, echoey voice', using short simple words in one-word sentences, that almost seep into our bones to make us feel the cold, eerie atmosphere: 'Cold. Ice. Iron'.

Also examine the highly evocative use of anonymous voices 'spoken quite matter-of-factly' in contrast to Tottie's strange and impassioned monologue to the baby in the next scene (Act Two, Scene Two). Why does Glover use this and what effect do you think is created here? What ideas are being suggested in this scene and how does this relate to the overall themes of the play? We also hear 'low whispery' anonymous voices in Act One, Scene Five when Tottie tells her story to the baby about the ghost up on the old rigs, almost as if they could be voices from the past, a sort of folk memory: the voice of the place and its people.

6. LANGUAGE, IMAGERY AND SYMBOLISM

Language

We have already noticed a number of parallels with Gibbon's *Sunset Song* and there are also interesting similarities and of course differences in the language of the two works. Though both appear to be mainly written in a Standard Scottish English, both create a distinctive Scots voice that brings their communities to life, as both writers skilfully weave into their English the vital ingredients of key Scots words and idioms, syntax, rhythms and rhymes. Thus both sound authentic while creating relatively few problems for those not familiar with Scots, once they have tuned in.

While Glover often manipulates Scots in a richly poetic way, she does not attempt to recreate actual Border Scots of the nineteenth century, but she deploys some archaisms or more old-fashioned Scots, such as 'lang syne rigs', 'sonsie' or 'puckle', to create a sense of the past. Yet her characters' speech and songs are rooted in a rural Scots, full of authentic idioms, still used throughout Scotland such as 'howk the tatties', 'shaw the neeps', 'drookit', 'mingin', 'girny', 'doesnae ken ought', 'bits o lassies', 'bung fu'', 'bide still'.

In fact there is a lot more Scots used than is apparent on the page simply because the key Scots words and idioms make us hear many surrounding words with a Scots pronunciation even though they are spelt in English, a linguistic legerdemain employed by Scottish writers since at least the eighteenth century. At the same time, as with Burns, we often have to ignore the spelling altogether, as the alliteration, assonance or rhyme indicate a word has to be said in Scots, such as in Tottie's rhyme in Act Two, Scene Five where 'dead' has to be said as 'deid' to rhyme with 'Tweed'.

There are also some important register contrasts used to show social differences, such as the subtle, but crucial language difference between the English of 'they know about turnips' and the much earthier Scots of 'we kenned about neeps' (Act One, Scene Two) which implies a sarcastic criticism of the gentry's knowledge of turnips being unrelated to the actual physical handling of them in the field i.e. they do not really know about them the way bondagers do. We also see the contrast between the way Ellen speaks to her former friends in Act One and her description of the way she speaks to the visitors in Act Two, showing not only the social gulf between the world of the field workers and the gentry, but also highlighting how Ellen has 'come up' in the world and perhaps the tensions she feels between her old and new identity. Probably the richest, and at times the most archaic Scots in the play is used by Tottie, for example in her conversations with the baby or in her repetition of bairn rhymes and songs, thereby suggesting an intuitive link to an ancient past via the traditional language of a childhood deeply rooted in her local community and culture.

While the language is rooted and earthy as befits the characters and the setting, it is at the same time, as in Gibbon, often very poetic and lyrical. We have already looked at how anonymous voices or choruses are used expressively throughout the play, as are songs and rhymes (see **Dramatic Technique and Style: Songs and rhymes**) but we can also see Glover's highly evocative poetic style at work if we examine some of the more reflective moments in the play, such as when we hear several characters talking about their past, for example Sara's vivid, poetic and very moving account of how she could not board the ship at Greenock or Ellen's passionate and dramatic description of how she won her way into the 'maister's bed' or Tottie's evocative and eerie account of what she heard and saw up on the 'lang syne rigs' on the moor (see **Characters and Themes: Tottie**). In passages like these Glover succeeds in creating dialogue which is not only highly lyrical, but vigorous and earthy at the same time, a powerful dramatic combination indeed.

Imagery and symbolism
Throughout the play, Glover's language is rich in imagery and we have also noted the use of recurring imagery related to weather, toil and bondage to the land and dirt, especially the repetition of the many different words for dung, while the alliterative antithesis of 'shoes shiny [...] shoothers dry' with

'soaked to the skin' sums up the contrast between mistress and bondager in two simple but effective visual images. In contrast to this we also find recurring references to shared, communal activities and celebrations, expressed via anonymous voices, ritual, movement, songs and dances, such as Liza and Ellen's shared description of the strange joy they discover in working the harvest and the kind of sexual energy and power they derive from it, something also depicted in Ellen's back-story about the kirn and capturing 'the maister' (both discussed in **Characters and Themes**).

In Act Two, Scene Three Ellen talks about how 'they made a lady of me' and confesses to the tell-tale signs of her pale face below her kerchief, but her cheeks and nose 'dirt brown', something that in the first year of her marriage betrayed the fact that she had been a bondager, whereas now she is 'all pale' and has become 'a proper lady'. While the contrast between the weather-beaten face of the bondager and the ladies smiling behind their fans vividly highlights the differences between the two ways of life, the contrasting symbolism of her brown and pale face also implies that there have been gains and losses for Ellen and that, in spite of all her new comforts and luxuries, perhaps she was healthier and happier as a bondager in some respects.

We have already commented on Glover's use of anonymous voices, sometimes operating like a chorus, to speak for the whole community, expressing both its shared culture and its collective or folk memory. Indeed the anonymous voices sometimes seem to be speaking to us from away back in the folk memory of the whole place, almost giving a voice to the place or to the land itself (Act Two, Scenes One and Two), something Gibbon also does in *Sunset Song*. Perhaps we could argue that it is through the use of folkloric and mythic elements that Glover raises her female protagonists to the level where their personal identities represent something larger than themselves.

Indeed, Glover seems to be elevating her women to a symbolic level where they could be seen as representing something universal and timeless. Her main characters can be viewed as archetypal figures, the mother, the young and innocent, the victim, the old woman, embodying the ancient and timeless experience of all women, experiencing love, loss and longing, but perhaps they can also be interpreted as metaphors for national identity or as symbolising the earth itself. Sara, who cannot leave Scotland to follow her wandering partner to Canada and whose daughter was begotten in the corn rigs, seems to embody something of the positive spirit of Scotland itself, a sort of mother earth figure, like Chris Guthrie in *Sunset Song*.

Women are closely linked to creation and fertility throughout the play or possess an intuitive earth knowledge and wisdom, so perhaps Tottie's abuse and incarceration due to the actions of men could be seen as symbolising the abuse or misuse of the earth itself by man. In fact Glover says in her introduction that Tottie stands for the land and Kello 'for our (sometimes criminal) carelessness'.

Imagery and symbolism related to clothing, props and appearance contribute a great deal to our understanding of character and theme and have already been discussed, but possibly the most powerful and haunting symbolism are those of the ghost on the 'lang syne rigs' up on the moors and the later warning of 'fields without folk'. This is discussed in the next chapter, along with the 'special plant' that nobody can now remember.

7. FURTHER DISCUSSION OF THEMES

Injustice, exploitation, victimisation

Glover depicts a world ill divided between the rich and the poor and focuses on the plight of the most vulnerable and exploited members of society, the marginalised, migrant female workers, with no protection, power or option other than work and marriage to a farm labourer who is himself poor and powerless. They are the victims of an unjust society which exploits its weakest as cheap labour but there are also several other kinds of injustice or victimisation in the play, affecting several characters, like Liza or the maister himself, but especially Tottie, the most vulnerable of all, who suffers a very cruel injustice. How does the author develop the theme of social division and inequality in the play? How does Steenie's letter imply what is wrong with Scotland?

Social and political change

Glover also raises the issue of social change and political agitation through Maister Elliott's political activities and his model farm. This also relates to the theme of female identity and the role of women; the argument amongst the women about bondagers and bairns raises the question of whether or not things have to be the way they have always been. What do we learn about their grievances in Act One, Scene Ten and what differences of opinion are expressed about what could be done to improve their lot? Who does not think that change is possible or required? Why? How are both the economic advantages and the human costs of 'progress' shown in Ellen's talk to the 'visitors' in Act Two, Scene Three? See also Steenie's letter in Act Two, Scene Seven.

Human dreams and hopes

Nothing turns out as expected or desired. In fact all the characters suffer a cruel disappointment in one way or another by the end and there is no security or permanence for bondagers, hind, master or mistress. Life is precarious and unpredictable: the Halloween predictions are all wrong, Kello is killed, Tottie locked up, no one is kept on and even the Elliotts lose their lease. In many ways the play illustrates the meaning of the lines about 'the best-laid schemes o' mice an men' from Burns' poem 'To a Mouse'. They do indeed 'gang aft agley' (often go wrong). Only those who have left Scotland seem to have found something better, as far as we can tell.

Female identity and the role of women

The play raises many issues about gender, identity, and discrimination in a very male-dominated, patriarchal society and explores the themes of change and challenge to conventional ways: the traditional role of marriage, motherhood, and conformity to society's norms (Maggie and Ellen to some extent) set against a rejection of this and a search for a new role (Liza) or alternatively a reconnection with older ways and customs that were less restrictive and prescriptive (Sara and Patie). The song 'Woo'd an married an a'' is used in Act One, Scene Four and repeated in Act Two, Scene Seven. Why would these women think that a bride would be so 'well off' in comparison with them? Are any of the married women in the play really so 'well off' or happy by the end? Remember that marrying for love has not always been the norm in human history, as in earlier times most people married for other reasons, such as security and protection, or money and property.

In letting her women tell their own story how well does Glover succeed in dramatising the plight of ignored and forgotten women in our history? What does the play say to you about what it was, or is, to be female, poor and Scottish? Do you think Glover is being over critical or negative about men?

Progress and human relationship to the land

At the end Sara repeats Tottie's stories about what she 'saw' up on the moors but also presents us with a vision of modern mechanised farming. Why do you think Glover gives Tottie the 'gift' of divination or second sight, of being able to see far back into the past and also into the future? Her vision about the man who came between her and the sun (Act Two, Scene Two) is repeated at the end of the play by her mother.

What do you think this vision is meant to suggest about the effects of technological progress on our way of life and environment?

What do you think the author is trying to convey to us via Tottie's vision about the man she met on the moor and the anonymous voices talking about 'the bread of carefulness' and 'the bread of progress'? Is her vision really about a future world of 'progress' and 'plenty'?

Or is Glover perhaps trying to warn us that there is a price to be paid for this 'plenty'? What is she suggesting about the consequences of human ignorance and detachment from the natural world or about our irresponsible and selfish destruction of the very planet that sustains us all? What idea is perhaps suggested by the man coming between Tottie and the sun?

Bondagers shows how the past is still alive in the present and suggests that we need to be attuned to our own past and to the natural world. If not, we will fail to learn those lessons which can give us a longer perspective and deeper vision than the short-sightedness of modern development, represented by the destruction of the special plants on the river embankment: 'Nobody thought to save any of the roots', and nobody can now remember what the plant was. Perhaps the forgotten plant symbolises something important that we ignore at our peril.

8. FURTHER READING

'Halloween', 'The Cottar's Saturday Night' and 'To a Mouse' by Robert Burns,
Selected poems of Marion Angus and Violet Jacob
The Cottagers of Glenburnie by Elizabeth Hamilton
Johnny Gibb of Gushetneuk by William Alexander
Sunset Song by Lewis Grassic Gibbon
Farmer's Boy by J. R. Allan
The Silver Darlings by Neil Gunn
The Quarry Wood by Nan Shepherd
Of Mice and Men by John Steinbeck
Another Time Another Place by Jessie Kesson
From Scenes Like These by Alan Sharp

9. THE STRAW CHAIR

Ideally you should read the play on your own first before working on it with others. As you study the play further, you might find it helpful to keep your own notes under the following headings:

- Setting and its influence on the characters (time period as well as place)
- Characters and relationships (especially how they change and develop)
- Plot (how the main conflicts are developed and resolved or not)
- Style and language (e.g. register, word choice, imagery, symbolism, tone)
- Dramatic technique (e.g. staging, acting, movement, sound and lighting)
- Themes
- Other interesting features

Brief synopsis
The play is set on the remote Hebridean island of Hirta (St Kilda) sometime between 1735 and 1740, during the period that Lady Rachel Grange was exiled there – probably because her husband, Lord Grange, feared she would reveal the political double-dealing of himself and other important members of the Scottish nobility. Lady Rachel is kept on the island virtually as a prisoner, but in the care of a Gaelic-speaking islander, Oona, who has little English. Aneas, a new minister from Edinburgh, who has never held a permanent post and who has just married a much younger wife, Isabel, has been sent to the island which has been without a minister for some time. Lady Rachel attempts to impose her social superiority on the new minister and his seventeen year old wife but when Rachel fails to impress them, she alternates between mockery and ingratiation. She needs their help in more ways than one, but as she makes no headway with the severely judgemental Aneas, she concentrates her attention on the naive Isabel. She also interferes in their relationship, even

trying to 'instruct' the innocent Isabel on the ways of men and on matters sexual. As a result, Aneas comes to see her as a thoroughly wicked woman and a bad influence on his young wife, but mainly due to Oona's influence, Isabel starts to see the island and even Lady Rachel in quite a different light. Instead of Aneas changing Hirta for the better, as he sees it, both he and his wife gradually fall under its spell and by the end, the island and its people have changed them both in a profoundly positive way. Lady Rachel desperately seeks Isabel's help in smuggling her letters to the mainland via a visiting ship, but Isabel, who has now taken pity on Lady Rachel, faces a difficult choice which may have dangerous and damaging consequences for herself and her husband.

10. COMMENTARY

Act One, Scene One

In the opening scene the author clearly emphasises the bareness and simplicity of life on Hirta. We are immediately struck by the bareness of the set. The only furniture is the bed, the lamp, a stool and a chest, and we soon learn that the island has few pots and only one chair. In fact, Aneas regards the present of the rough wooden stool as 'a triumph'. In this opening scene Rachel wears island dress, which is very simple, while the island's staple diet is sea birds and their eggs.

Our attention is also focused on the relationship between Isabel and Aneas and their different reasons for coming here. We can see immediately that they are ill at ease with each other, she is upset and feeling unwell and he does not know what to say or how to comfort her. He has come to the island as a summer missionary, to do God's work, and she feels it is her duty to support her husband, but she also thought it would be 'an adventure', never having left Edinburgh before. Yet we can see that the minister's young wife, who is only seventeen and only married ten days ago, is filled with dismay at the bleakness of the island, especially how primitive their 'manse' is, when actually it is the best house on the island. She feels she should never have come and despairs about coping with the islanders, especially Rachel. She prays to God to deliver her home safely to Edinburgh as 'speedily as possible'.

In contrast, our first impressions of Rachel are probably not very favourable and we are unlikely to see her as very sympathetic to the younger woman. She is very abrupt, bad-tempered, arrogant and snobbish, clearly regarding herself as superior to all the 'fools' on the island. She appears quite intimidating to Isabel who is upset by her manner and her comments about the islanders and this makes her despair even further, as we see from her prayer.

On the other hand, we are much more likely to see Aneas in a positive light. He appears to be very calm and patient with Isabel, he has a strong sense of his calling, seems sincere about what he is doing and is considerate towards others. Above all, he does not mind the hardships and he also tries hard to cheer Isabel up. By the end of the scene he is partly successful in this, as we see in the way he is uplifted by the words of the psalm and tries to find comfort in this for her. In response, she tries to smile, even makes a joke about their situation and she takes his hand to go down to lead the prayers for Captain Martin and his crew. By the end of the scene, we perhaps feel that things might not turn out so bleakly for her after all, though clearly many difficulties lie ahead.

Act One, Scene Two
In the second scene, Glover reveals more about Rachel's attitude towards Oona and the people of Hirta, but we also see how her manner changes dramatically once Isabel arrives. At first she treats Oona as an idiotic servant, hurling insults and accusations at her and she despises the islanders as 'fools'. However, when Isabel calls she starts to behave like a grand lady, 'imperiously' offering the younger woman her hand, thereby clearly trying to establish her superior status. Rachel at first acts the part of the society hostess, trying to impress the younger woman with her rich and powerful connections and boasting of her fame as a great beauty (Rachel, Jacob's wife in the Old Testament, was a famous beauty). She clearly displays her superiority to the minister's wife, but notice how her questions are also probing to find out how Isabel might be useful to her. Rachel tells Isabel how she was forcibly abducted by Lord Lovat and McLeod's servants, robbed, and kept on the island against her will. She also tells her that she tried to get a message to the boat that brought Aneas and Isabel, but Oona, who is her 'jailor', forced her back.

However, she is also rude and disparaging towards Isabel ('He seems an old man' [...] 'You are not very pretty') as well as trying to frighten her ('The mice grow big as rats here [...] this is a hellish, stinking isle'). Yet she also becomes very agitated and angry when recounting her abduction, behaving more like the mad wretch we saw earlier, before

again reverting to her 'drawing-room manner' as Oona leads
her away: 'I pray you make my compliments to the minister
– until we should meet'. Thus her manner changes quickly
and unexpectedly, revealing how volatile she is.

In contrast, Isabel treats Oona with respect, never as a
servant, always as an equal, but she shows a deferential
attitude towards Rachel at first, as we see from the way she
curtsies and calls her 'my lady'. She is clearly intimidated by
Rachel but also rather shocked by her very blunt comments
and questions. She even feels a bit afraid of her, as we see
when she moves towards her. She clearly thinks she might
be dangerous and indeed she confesses to Aneas that 'she
frightens me a little. A lot!'. Isabel really does not know quite
what to make of her, but she does show some concern for her,
as we see when she asks 'who did this?' (halfway through
this scene) and when she tells Aneas, shortly after, 'she goes
mad. And so should if I were abducted to this place'.

In support of Isabel's impression of her, we hear what
Rachel says to Oona and see the way she treats her. Early
in the scene, she calls Oona's porridge 'heathen slops'. She
grabs the bowl from her and it ends up on the ground, something Oona regards as a terrible waste. Rachel then calls her
'a thief' and tells Isabel that Oona has stolen her jewels but
when Oona leads her away she accuses her of trying to starve
her, claiming, 'You have given me nothing to eat!'. Thus we can
see she is unreliable and possibly liable to exaggeration and
distortion. Yet Oona keeps a watchful eye on her throughout,
ignores all her insults and taunts and keeps trying to calm
her down. She also tells her she has done enough talking for
now, that she must eat and then sleep and finally tries to
lead her away from Isabel, as if she might harm her, almost
like a warder looking out for the danger signs.

We also see Aneas's mood contrasted with Isabel's in
this scene. While Isabel is clearly stunned by her meeting
with Rachel, Aneas has had 'an invigorating morning – in
his own sober way', and is clearly exhilarated by his tour of
the island, having met everyone and declaring excitedly 'I
have never seen such a place'. His description of being on top
of Conachair shows that he has not just been climbing the

heights, but is on a spiritual high as he sounds as if he has been in heaven looking down on the whole world. However Isabel does not respond to his mood as she is not listening, but is instead 'brooding' over her 'Hirta and its highest born inhabitant' (Rachel), and we are later told that while 'he is lost in wonder', she is 'lost in thought'. When she suddenly starts asking him about Edinburgh oyster cellars, he is 'perplexed by the change of subjects' as we imaginatively plunge from the cliffs of Hirta to the cellars of the city, from the heights to the depths as it were, and aspects of city life the innocent Isabel knows little or nothing about.

Yet their conversation about Edinburgh is not merely some kind of diversion as it reveals a great deal about Isabel and her upbringing. She has had a very sheltered, strict and restricted life, as she has had to act as mother to her uncle's large family from quite a young age, with no experience of the social life of the city, but she is curious about many of the things Rachel talked about, the forbidden aspects of city life her uncle disapproved of, especially oyster cellars, assemblies and dancing and we see how there is a fun-loving and possibly rebellious side to her as we learn how she and her niece danced reels and jigs in the kitchen without her uncle knowing.

Glover also stresses how Isabel and Aneas differ strongly in their attitudes towards the problem of the 'mad woman'. In spite of being shocked and disturbed by Rachel and what she has heard, Isabel is sympathetic and anxious to do what she can for this strange woman. Isabel therefore seems trusting and kindly, if somewhat naive. Whereas she is inclined to believe Rachel's story because 'she told me so', his view is that she is mad and you 'cannot tell the truth of what she says'. He doesn't appear very interested in Rachel and her problems and even thinks that her exile on Hirta may be a 'gentle Bedlam' as opposed to being locked up in a city madhouse.

We can also see a tension developing between them over this issue by the end of the scene. While she takes pity on Rachel and feels it is their Christian duty to try to help this poor woman, he is wary of becoming involved in some-

thing that he feels a minister should have nothing to do
with, because it may be delicate or even dangerous and he
is actually rather annoyed with his wife for asking him to
help this mad woman. He reminds her quite firmly that as
the minister's wife she 'will conduct herself accordingly' and
that, although Rachel's soul may be his concern, why she
is there is none of his business and he cuts Isabel off quite
abruptly with 'she is McLeod's business. And the Steward's'.
After what he clearly regards as his last word on the matter,
we see how he 'distances himself' and, rather ironically, sits
down to open his Bible, which is of course supposed to teach
us about such qualities as compassion for others and forgiveness. Her disappointment and frustration indicate that she
feels this should be his concern and that we have not heard
the last word on the matter.

Act One, Scene Three
In this scene we learn more about Oona and the differences
between her way of life and those of the mainland. She is
always busy, especially looking after Rachel, but she seems
endlessly patient and never complains. She has only left
the island once, when she and her husband accompanied a
minister and his wife on a visit to Skye, where she learned
English, though she thinks she could never learn to read or
write and is in awe of the minister for being able to turn
'black marks' on paper into words. We learn more about the
islanders' diet and storing their eggs as opposed to eating
them fresh and how Oona, on a visit to the Isle of Skye, was
amazed and amused by the luxurious lifestyle of that island's
gentry who waste good cloth on tapestries and wear shoes
every day, leaving them with 'soft and silly' feet. Yet she was
also amazed and moved by the beauty of the trees and the
spirits whispering sadly in the woods of Skye and she feels
pity for Lowlanders who do not have spirits. Obviously she
sees no contradiction in believing in both a pagan goddess
and a Christian God. She appears a genuinely good-natured,
wise, patient and kindly person, though, like all the islanders, she is very superstitious.

Glover clearly wishes Isabel to develop a deeper apprecia-
tion of the islanders and their way of life and so she lets her
see things through Oona's eyes, as opposed to the prejudiced
views of the outsiders, especially Rachel. Note that the name
Oona in Gaelic is simply the same as Una in English, which
is Latin for 'who is one', a name of Hebrew origin. Perhaps
the choice of this name is meant to suggest what a unique
individual she is, quite unlike anyone Isabel has encountered
before, but also maybe the idea of someone who is completely
at one with her island, in harmony with her people and her
place, seeing it as 'the sweetest place on earth'.

Yet we also see that the islanders have a rather ambivalent attitude towards Rachel. They view her as 'the guest' of
Lord McLeod of Skye and it is therefore their duty to look
after her, but they also see her as a 'great skua', a piratical
and parasitical bird they cannot be rid of which bullies, robs
and feeds off other birds, so they see her as an ill omen, a
bringer of bad luck.

Notice how immediately after Isabel's conversation with
Oona, Glover brings in Rachel to give us a very different
perspective on Hirta. We now hear the bitter views of the
aristocratic woman who has been used to all the luxuries of
life but who is being held here against her will. She sees the
island as a 'stinking' hell on earth, 'one great God-forsaken sin'.
We might understand why Rachel feels this way because of
her background and what has happened to her, but because
she is so disrespectful to Oona, who remains uncomplaining and dignified, we are more likely to share Oona's view-
point, as Isabel increasingly does. About half way through
the scene, Rachel calls Isabel a 'hypocrite' as she feels Isabel
is not being sincere, only trying to be nice to Oona.

In contrast, Isabel tries to be kind and supportive to both
of them, not wanting to take sides, as we see when she is
supportive of Oona in her defence of the island, but also
when she tries to comb Rachel's hair and takes pity on her
by kneeling beside her, holding her hand, thus demonstrat-
ing to the audience that she is a very tactful, considerate and
sympathetic person.

However, when Aneas enters we see that he clearly does not share his wife's sympathies for Rachel. The stage directions tell us that he is 'rigid with righteousness', possibly about the way she is dressed, but certainly about the conversation he has just overheard in which Rachel speaks venomously about her children and her unfaithful husband. Whereas she immediately reverts to being the charming hostess, he speaks to her very formally, his answers are curt and he quickly cuts her off when she tries to tell him about her troubles. We are told that Rachel is 'pathetically discomfited', and there is an 'awkward silence'. He then fails to respond to Isabel's plea for compassion and starts to question Rachel in a rather accusatory manner about her non-attendance at church, offering her only rather cold ministerial support by way of prayers in English and a spare Bible. Thus Aneas sees this 'wicked' woman as a dangerous influence on Isabel.

Unfortunately, Rachel has made a big effort to impress the new minister, by dressing up in her tattered Edinburgh gown, ironically almost the very first thing Aneas disapproves of as she is 'revealing an embarrassing amount of flesh'. We can see how 'discomfited' she is by his manner and that she is extremely disappointed by his treatment of her. She sees his 'help' as an example of 'rigid piety', displaying an outward show of being very holy. He appears more concerned about the formalities of conventional religious worship and finding fault with her for her failings, rather than trying to understand her problems or offering her any real help.

Isabel, however, is disappointed by Aneas's attitude. We are told she is 'discomfited on Rachel's behalf' and 'wants Aneas to make amends', though she can sense his anger with both of them. She then moves closer to him, pleading with him 'for compassion' via words and looks, repeating his name 'Aneas! … Aneas!'. Yet he cannot bring himself to respond to her plea in a sympathetic manner and at the end of the scene we sense the tension between them as they watch Rachel go.

At the end of the scene, the singing of a psalm not only links in with the worship Aneas has been questioning Rachel about, but also reminds us of the very genuine devotion of the islanders and the communal culture they share, which neither Rachel nor the minister are part of, just at the very moment he fails to show any sympathy for a lost soul, someone sorely needing his help.

Act One, Scene Four
Whereas in Scene Three, Rachel was 'grotesquely, sadly garbed' in the gown she was wearing when she was carried off from Edinburgh, we now see that Isabel is not wearing her shoes and stockings, items of dress that would be essential for any respectable lady in Edinburgh. Her removal of them suggests she is possibly rejecting her old identity in order to identify with the islanders, something that would have been inconceivable when she first arrived.

We are also shown that Isabel and Aneas have differing attitudes towards the culture of the islanders. Whereas she found his prayers very long, she loves their singing for 'truly reaching up to heaven', but he is shocked and saddened by their belief about 'scales' covering the first humans, something he sees as a blasphemy that will deprive them of salvation. Ironically his religion's truths are just as superstitious as the islanders' ideas about creation. She is literally and metaphorically in tune with the islanders and he is not.

Although Isabel started off regretting her decision to come here, she is now increasingly receptive and sympathetic to Hirta's culture and wants to change to fit in with the islanders' ways. By contrast, he started off being enthusiastic about his work and the island itself, but, since he sees it as his job to correct the islanders' erroneous beliefs, he now realises that he faces an uphill struggle. He is being much more critical than sympathetic, and with Rachel he is very judgemental indeed, dismissing her as a 'godless, mischievous, evil creature [...] nothing better than a strumpet' and ordering his wife not to speak to her again. Notice her 'mutinous pause' after being warned again not to speak to her which drives Isabel to ask him the very question he should be asking himself: 'You will minister to eighty odd islanders, and ignore the one soul who needs you?'.

In her willingness to take pity on Rachel, Isabel shows herself to be a better Christian than her husband, the minister, and she also shows how acutely perceptive she is in her observation that the islanders 'will pray and praise till dawn. Whether there is minister or no. But the Lady Rachel hides in the shadows outside'. Isabel is also prepared to defy her husband's order, firstly because it is impractical and secondly because she feels it is cruel. In addition we see her 'mutinous pause' and her failure to follow his instructions to put out the light, a very significant visual image which reflects the growing tension between them, though Aneas is too tired to argue further and drifts off to sleep.

Glover frequently deploys folklore and song in her work and here the ballad of 'The Demon Lover' is used to suggest that Rachel sees a parallel between the fate of the woman in the song and her own i.e. being deceived by a devil in disguise, the lover or husband who wants rid of her. She obviously equates being taken to Hirta with hell, the destination of the woman in the ballad. She is also trying to warn Isabel about how deceitful men can be and how best to keep them – something she has not been too successful at herself.

Nevertheless, Rachel does manage to get Isabel to confess to having problems in her relationship with Aeneas. She asks some very frank questions, very loudly, knowing that Isabel does not want to waken her husband, thereby almost blackmailing her into answering and, when she walks away after giving some very blunt advice, she taunts her by calling her 'rigidly pious' which provokes Isabel into a more open and honest answer. In the face of Rachel's persistent questioning, Isabel is forced to confess that, although she does want Aneas, he does not seem to desire her, being too busy with 'sanctification of the spirit' to have time for any sexual pleasure and so has not 'tried' her yet. This makes their bed a cold, damp place, the marriage clearly not having been consummated. Rachel mocks Isabel for having water in her veins instead of blood and gives her some very frank and physical advice indeed: 'hoist up your semmit', 'take him to bed [...] Accost him! Stroke him! [...] Bite him!'.

This conversation clearly reveals a warmer relationship developing between the two women. Rachel provokes Isabel into talking very openly and frankly as woman-to-woman and, although she taunts Isabel, when she sees how confused she is, the cynical Rachel takes pity on her and gives her more sisterly advice. Although this shocks her, it actually makes her laugh and they go on to laugh even more at Rachel's story about how Lord Grange 'got bit on the bum'. A real friendship is starting to take root here as they laugh like two naughty girls, while Isabel also surprises Rachel, not only by her openness and honesty, but in the way she is much less deferential and now stands up to her.

We have already heard Oona likening Rachel to the great skua and, when the latter spots it, she calls it 'a devil [...] in the sky'. This is echoed in Oona's description of it as 'the imp of hell' and Isabel is 'surprised by the hate in her voice' when she explains what they will do to it if they catch it. Rachel clearly feels the whole world has turned against her, including the people of Hirta. We could read this as implying that, in her own warped way, this is how she wants to see herself, as she is watching it 'with admiration', thereby identifying herself, as the outsider, with the bird the islanders hate. However at this point she is mocking the islanders' superstitions, from sacred wells to devil birds, and therefore she could also be mocking them because they see her as the devil bird. Yet even though Oona is 'watching it with hate', she does not seem to have Rachel in mind when she speaks of the skua this time, no matter how much Rachel has been mocking their beliefs.

By the end of Act One the mood again changes dramatically. Isabel joins in the islanders' excitement about the arrival of the Steward, an event eagerly anticipated by everyone, as nine couples, a highly auspicious number, are to be married when he arrives, so there will be much to celebrate and Isabel is clearly keen to take part in this celebration. Yet, in being excited about the arrival of the Steward, Isabel feels a bit guilty, almost as if she is letting her new 'friend' down because Rachel has no reason to celebrate the arrival of someone she regards as 'a maggoty liar'.

Act Two, Scene One
In contrast to Isabel's despair in the opening scene, we now

hear lively dance music and shouting offstage before she appears and when she enters she is now wearing island clothes, waving her shawl above her head, singing and dancing barefoot, clearly playing a full part in the wedding celebrations, a very dramatic contrast to her mood at the start of the play. Obviously the island way of life is beginning to affect her and she is exhilarated by the wedding celebrations, something we soon learn more about during this scene. Glover clearly wants us to concentrate on the effect the weddings have had on Isabel and Aneas, rather than the event itself, a very important reason for not dramatising the actual wedding, apart from the fact that this would mean a larger cast.

However, Rachel soon intervenes to spoil their mood as she finds much to laugh at in the behaviour of the minister and his wife, but her laughter seems insensitive and cruel. Calling Isabel and Aneas 'rigidly pious raggedy dolls' shows she thinks they are both spineless creatures, too strictly religious to actually enjoy making love, like lifeless puppets with no blood in their veins. However, she has been pleasantly surprised to discover that there is more to Isabel than she at first thought. Isabel is outraged by Rachel spying on them and replies to her mockery very angrily and defiantly, clearly surprising, but also impressing Rachel by how much fight and spirit she shows. We are now seeing a greatly changed Isabel from the despairing, hysterical girl we saw at the beginning of the play – very far indeed from 'the raggedy doll' that Rachel thought she was.

Rachel needs to change the subject at this point and cunningly detains Isabel to bring the conversation round to a letter seeking help from her cousin which she needs to be smuggled on board the Steward's ship. Isabel's joyfulness has obviously reminded Rachel of the intense excitement she experienced when she first fell in love, though perhaps she is indirectly trying to warn Isabel about how fickle and despicable men can be once they have had their way, but Rachel also needs to win the sympathy of the younger woman to persuade her to help her. Telling Isabel about the 'honey times' of her own courtship and her cruel descent into a 'raggedy doll' also

provides a stark dramatic contrast between her sophisticated, but corrupt Edinburgh society and the much simpler
life on Hirta and the communal wedding celebrations which
have so exhilarated Isabel.

In order to persuade Isabel to take her letter, Rachel firstly
tries to regain her sympathy which she has just lost, then
tries to persuade her that she is within her rights, that it
can do no harm since she is only writing to her cousin and it
can easily be hidden, but she then uses emotional pressure
by appealing to Isabel's conscience about how much she has
suffered and Isabel is the only one who can help her. She
finally resorts to desperate pleading, grabbing hold of Isabel
'fiercely' and thrusting the letter into her hand just before
Oona arrives.

Although she did not have much choice, accepting the
letter leaves Isabel with a real dilemma, a test of conscience,
and she cannot confide in anyone about it. Only she can
resolve this, but she is very unsure of what is the right thing
to do: torn between helping Rachel and having to deceive her
husband, but also doing something that could lead to trouble
for him as well as for Oona. As we see her standing 'guiltily'
fingering the letter, wondering what to do, we realise that
this is a real moment of crisis for Isabel, very much a turning
point in her character development and in the plot, as her
decision could have far-reaching consequences.

There is also the possibility, only a hint, that Oona suspects
that the letter is not Isabel's, as she 'peruses it closely' perhaps
only reflecting her fascination with the mystery of writing,
but also maybe hinting at a sub-textual level (i.e. reading
between the lines, not stated but shown in other ways, such
as looks or tone) that she is trying to warn Isabel but cannot
speak about it explicitly. We are left wondering whether
Isabel will or will not take the letter and whether she will be
caught and what the consequences might be: something that
seems harmless enough but is in fact full of hidden dangers
and far-reaching consequences.

Notice how effectively the author uses music and voices
offstage at the beginning and end of this scene. The wild
dance music and shouts of the dancers, which set the mood

of celebration at the start, quicken at the end of this scene
in step with Isabel's quickening heartbeat and the tension
building within her, as well as the increase in suspense and
the general excitement of the whole community. It then
slowly fades into a 'quieter air' to provide a link into the
next scene and the mellower sleepy mood after three days'
celebrations.

Act Two, Scene Two
At the start of this scene we focus on how the wedding celebrations have affected Isabel and Aneas. He is obviously
anxious about the social proprieties of the occasion, worried
that his wife did not show the Steward the proper respect, as
she would have been expected to dance with him, or maybe
he is disappointed that she missed an opportunity to make a
favourable impression on a man of influence and power. We
also see that they are both still a bit awkward and shy, but
Isabel is lively and garrulous, as we see from her nervous
chatter, full of short, incomplete sentences and her struggle
to find the right words, whereas Aneas is at first a bit stiff
and formal, talking about the Steward, but he is also apolo-
getic and nervous, trying to interrupt her flow of words to
apologise, though he gradually mellows to become more
gentle, affectionate, and tender, eventually talking much
more freely, openly and honestly.

They are now trying to talk to each other more openly, if
somewhat awkwardly, to apologise to each other for their
first faltering sexual experience, fearing that they have
disappointed each other, but we can see from their nervous-
ness that they now clearly both desire each other and we see
a new tenderness and intimacy just beginning to blossom. No
doubt the wedding celebrations played an important part,
especially all the music and dancing and the fun involved,
a sort of communal quickening of the pulse, leading to their
'walk' up to the cleits.

We also see Aneas in quite a new light in this scene. With
surprising honesty, he confesses to watching the beautiful
girl and how she aroused his desire for Isabel, an experience that seems to have helped thaw him out! He has always

been kind and considerate towards her, but we now see a new frankness, along with a loving tenderness and desire stirring within him, leading to the moment of intimacy that is so rudely interrupted by Rachel's presence. Thus we start to see him as a warmer, more sympathetic and more complex human being here, not just as a man with a mission, dedicated to his 'calling'.

Unfortunately, the discovery of Rachel in the bed suddenly and dramatically reverses the mood from the tender love scene to a moment of real surprise and shock that again leads on to anger and tension between the couple. Yet there is also a cruelly humorous undercurrent, as the loving couple, full of nervous sexual anticipation, suddenly find a drunken and cheeky old hag falling out of their bed – not everyone's idea of a honeymoon surprise, and certainly not the minister's!

As we see from her abrupt commands and clenched teeth and in the way she firmly tries to steer Rachel out the door, Isabel now shows no sign of her former deference and respect towards her ladyship. On the other hand, Aneas is left 'speechless', 'furious', 'bitter' and 'humiliated', leaving Isabel not daring to look or speak to him, especially after Rachel has teased Isabel very cheekily, offered her a very bawdy honeymoon benediction and then repeated the bleating noise as she departs. This is rather a cruel and insensitive piece of mockery, something Rachel seems unable to resist, indicating her contempt for Aneas and the pious religiosity he seems to stand for. She still sees him as a small-minded, cowardly hypocrite, but perhaps there is also an element of jealous rivalry for Isabel's love and attention about her mockery.

After Rachel departs, Aneas speaks to Isabel very abruptly and coldly: ordering her to bed like a naughty child, blaming her for what has happened, thinking she has been confiding in and scheming with this mad, wicked woman. Yet, we see him relenting a bit at the end, as he tries to calm down, perhaps feeling a little guilty about what he has said, but when he gets into bed he turns his face to the wall to show his displeasure with her. While his fury over what has happened is perhaps understandable, blaming Isabel is not, but we have to realise how humiliated and stung he is by the thought that his wife has been scheming and 'snickering' at him behind his back. Isabel is obviously stung by being falsely accused and hurt by his lack of understanding and trust, but also disappointed that the wedding celebrations have not ended as she hoped. She shows this by sitting 'hunched' on the bed, being left 'perched' on the edge, getting sulkily into it and banging the bed door angrily to let us see the frustration and anger she cannot put into words.

When Aneas calls Rachel a Pandarus at the end of the scene, this is really quite an obscure reference to classical mythology which not only indicates how bookish he is, but also underlines their difficulties in understanding each other. At first glance, 'Pandarus' does not seem to fit the context as well as 'Pandora', the Greek Eve and source of all evils, and calling her this would show that Aneas means Rachel is a mischief-maker, the source of all their troubles on this island. However, Pandarus, the uncle of Cressida, was a go-between or procurer in a treacherous love intrigue in the story of Troilus and Cressida, a popular medieval tale set during the Trojan wars which Shakespeare used for one of his darkest tragedies. Since 'Pandora' is a much more widely understood reference, Glover clearly wants Aneas to use a reference that probably only a classical scholar would understand, to suggest that Aneas regards Rachel as a deceitful procuress. Glover uses this obscure reference to suggest that, although he is much more learned, his learning is all from reading books, not from life, so maybe he is not as clever as he thinks he is in terms of reading people's characters, as is clearly evident from the way he is so unfair to Isabel here. At the same time, if he is so very wrong about his own wife, he is quite possibly also wrong about Rachel.

Act Two, Scene Three

This is the longest and arguably the most important scene in the play. It is also very important in terms of character development, relationships, plot and theme.

Again the mood at the start of this scene contrasts dramatically with the previous one. We can see from the way they talk about the weather and Isabel going to Boreray that there is no sign that they are still annoyed with each other and, although he is dismissive about her desire to go there, it seems more out of concern for her safety. When they talk further about Hirta, she is very supportive and reassuring when he expresses his feelings of inadequacy about his work on the island and this leads on to him talking in a very affectionate way about how he was first attracted to her. He then confesses that he 'could not find the words' to speak of his love for her till he came to Hirta, and at this point they look at each other lovingly, 'last night's anger healed'. Therefore they both show a willingness to forgive and forget, not allowing any negative feelings to be carried over from the previous night, thereby revealing their growing love for each other.

How much he is changing is also shown by the fact that he is now full of admiration for the strength and sincerity of the islanders' faith which he sees as 'steady as the rock they live on', offering him 'a lesson in humility'. He is beginning to realise that, although they have had little scriptural instruction from missionaries like him, he has more to learn from them than they have from him. We also see Isabel's growing love for the island and its people, as we see when Aneas says he is glad she loves Hirta, and her answer is a very emphatic: 'Oh I do'. This is further emphasised in the repetition of her fervent desire to go with the young women to Boreray: 'I would so love to go' and later 'I would so like to go'. She now regards them as her friends, in fact the first friends she has ever had, reminding us of how her own adolescence had been taken from her by having to look after all her uncle's children. At this point she starts pleading with him to let her go to Boreray, like a little girl asking a big favour from her father.

When, however, he asks who has put the idea into her head, we immediately see that he still does not really trust her and is suspicious that it was Rachel's doing. When Isabel tries to defend Rachel, he shows how convinced he is that she is a very dangerous influence on Isabel, by warning his wife that Rachel is 'the devil', 'satanic', 'the skua', thus revealing that his superstitions are much more harmful than the islanders'. He thinks Isabel is too naive but when she continues defending Rachel, he reprimands his wife for being 'thrawn' and warns her of 'the danger of being too trouble-some a wife' and even accuses her of starting to sound like Rachel, unaware of the irony that he is accusing his wife of the very thing Rachel's husband accused her of. Isabel is so 'frightened' and 'wounded' by his attitude that she calls him 'a hypocrite' because she feels that he is not really a good Christian for demonising the very person most in need of his help and compassion, Rachel.

Is Isabel just being impulsive, naive and 'thrawn' or is he being too judgemental, too self-righteous and hypocritical? Certainly Rachel is causing them both problems and she is scheming, but Aneas makes some very harsh judgements of both Rachel and his wife here. Yet as soon as Isabel calls him a 'hypocrite', we see she regrets it and moves away, just at the very moment we see him moving towards her, wanting to speak to her, but she is unaware of this. We are shown how much she is suffering from the bitter words she utters and also by the stage directions telling us she is 'hunched and miserable, divided between indignation and tears', but she also feels very angry and resentful about what he has said. He, on the other hand, simply 'can't cope with this' and exits.

Ironically, Isabel's quote from the Old Testament Book of Proverbs is all about the importance of a wife's love and loyalty towards her husband, something of which Isabel feels she must remind herself. This is Isabel's lowest point emotion-ally in the play: torn between loyalty to him as a dutiful wife and her concern for Rachel, and she is distraught about the fact that this is causing trouble between them. Notice that as she reaches the line in the proverb about stretching out her hands to the poor and needy and speaking with a kindly tongue, Rachel enters, immediately wanting to know whether Isabel has hidden the letter.

Yet, in spite of this gulf between them, when Rachel calls Aneas a 'stickit' minister (i.e. stuck, failed, unsuccess-ful) Isabel immediately tries to defend him. Although she adamantly insists that he is 'not stickit, not in any way' and that 'he is a very good minister', her honesty forces her to admit that he is only secretary to the secretary of the Society for the Propagation of Christian Knowledge, deliberately using its long and important sounding title to make Aneas sound important. When she adds that 'he is to get a living soon' (i.e. a church of his own) she cannot say when or where, only that 'he hasn't yet decided', or to be more honest, he has not got a job at all and was probably only offered this temporary post in Hirta because they could not get anyone else to go there.

However, Rachel's attitude towards the other two women changes in this scene in a most surprising way. After cunningly detaining Isabel to find out about the letter and being dismissive towards Oona as usual, she gradually exerts her charm to beguile and cajole the other women into drinking with her, especially the very reluctant Oona, though note that Isabel 'suddenly, vehemently' snatches the bottle from Rachel, almost as an act of rebellion or release for her pent-up anger. Thus the other two are gradually 'lulled by her mildness' and 'pleasantness', behaviour that is most out of character for this sharp-tongued, bitter woman. While Rachel desperately needs Isabel and Oona's help, sharing the brandy certainly helps to break down barriers between them and the three women become much more sympathetic towards each other, as they share stories, sorrows and laughter, argue, quarrel and even fight with each other.

Notice how by the end of this scene, Rachel shows concern for Isabel by shouting after her that she will need her shawl and we see how her view of Isabel has shifted very significantly in her ironic and understated comment after she has gone: 'queer bit of a lass! May never worse be among us!'. In addition, she also shows a much kindlier attitude to Oona, by proposing a toast to Boreray and helping the drunken Oona down the path, a role reversal we could not have imagined earlier. This long scene is presented as a female bonding session that throws up quite a few surprises and secrets and also changes their relationships and even their lives, particularly Isabel's.

This scene also shows the old deferential and respectful Isabel disappearing and being replaced by a much tougher, more rebellious young woman. In contrast to the Isabel who sits, albeit reluctantly, when told to do so by Rachel near the start of this scene, we see her character, which has been slowly evolving up to this stage, undergoing a dramatic transformation. Stung by Rachel's mockery and also 'intoxicated' by the brandy, Isabel bluntly tells her to shut her 'gob' and even wrestles her chair from her, leaving her flat on her back. She is also determined to fight for her right to be herself and shape her own future, a character development which is central to the theme of the play. Thus she becomes determined to prove Rachel wrong and defy her husband, by running down and trying to jump into the boat at the very last minute. However, she has to be 'lifted' out of the waves and into the boat by the women, an action that shows how much she needs the help and support of others, but this act of rebellion profoundly affects her life and her relationship with Aneas.

We also learn much more in this scene about Oona as a woman: the joys and sorrows she has experienced through her genuine love for her husband and grief for his loss. At the same time we also learn much more about love and marriage customs on the island, especially the dangerous courtship ordeal that young men have to pass – standing on one foot on the ledge of the Lovers' Crag – all of which provides a very sharp and very telling contrast to the far more dangerous and poisonous behaviour of a sophisticated Edinburgh society that Rachel appears to be a victim of.

In some ways the three women can be seen as representing the different strands of Scottish society: the upper class, the middle class and the common people. They also represent three sharply contrasting universal female experiences in their relationships with men: Rachel, the betrayed and rejected wife; Oona, the widow, whose love is deep and enduring; and Isabel, the innocent newlywed struggling to make a marriage work. This pivotal scene reveals how much they have in common as women, in spite of all the things that keep them apart.

If we compare the different attitudes expressed by Aneas, Rachel and Oona about Isabel's decision to go to Boreray we can see how they affect her decision to go. Aneas has firmly told her she cannot go, firstly because he fears for her safety, but also because he is unhappy about her making plans to go without telling him. He reminds her 'your place is here with me', but he is also suspicious and angry because he thinks that Rachel has put the idea into her head. In fact Rachel belittles and taunts her cruelly at this point by calling her 'Isabella Hum Drum! Isabella Miss the boat!' and mocking her chances of getting any bairn 'from the stickit Minister!'. Yet perhaps she is trying to taunt her into proving her wrong, as well as provoking her into defying her husband. She certainly succeeds in rousing her fighting spirits, so that her rebellious mood and anger, plus a drop or two of brandy, make her all the more determined to prove both of them wrong.

Oona is in fact the only one who thinks going to Boreray is a good idea as Aneas will miss her all the more, something that will be very good for her marriage, like the island women whose babies are born nine months after going there. Undoubtedly Isabel's desire for an adventure, the freedom and friendship that accompanies it, and the belief that it might transform her marriage are all very positive and powerful motives behind her passionate desire to go to Boreray.

Act Two, Scene Four
This short, but very important scene focuses our attention on the relationship between Aneas and Rachel. When he finds her trying to break into the kist, he is cold, critical and hostile, abruptly ordering her home and trying to excuse himself, but we can see he is also unsure of how to deal with her by his offer to pray for her and telling her to repent. Finally he loses patience, starts to reprimand her for being 'an uncomfortable wife' and tells her that 'it is no accident you were set on Hirta! It is a remedy!'. He is obviously unaware of how ironic his condemnation is. She also stares coldly at him, but then laughs wryly at being told to go 'home' and scorns his offers to pray, asking him, 'are you never done praying?'. Finally she appeals to God to save her from 'little Ministers', thus belittling his piety as pointless and petty.

When Rachel imagines he is Lord Grange, she berates him for all his betrayal, deception and cruelty, like a disturbed

woman reliving her suffering in front of our eyes. This is a
very dramatic way of making him see into Rachel's mind,
leaving him visibly shaken by what he has seen and heard
and beginning to doubt 'what is true and who are guilty'. He
then almost forgets she is there as he wrestles with his own
conscience, recognising his blindness and his uncertainties
about what he is doing here, asking God for guidance. When
she comes out of her fit, Aneas almost has to remind himself,
as well as her, who they are and where they are. He attempts
to reassert himself by ordering her to go and find Oona, but
she does not recognise him as 'Missionary to Hirta', only
'Isabella's mannikin! The raggedy doll!'.

When Rachel leaves we are told 'he does not even notice'
as he is 'sunk in his own despair' and starts praying desperately for Isabel's safety, asking to be forgiven for his own sins
and not to be punished for this. We might feel that his judgemental attitude and lack of compassion towards Rachel, plus
his unjust accusations and lack of understanding of his wife,
have brought this on himself and maybe he deserves to suffer,
but his first concern at this point is for his wife, while he is at
least accepting that he has sinned and is beginning to recognise that he may have been in the wrong about many things.

This scene marks a crucial turning point in the drama.
Firstly Aneas is shocked by Rachel speaking to him as if
he is Lord Grange, then he is given the shock news about
the letter having been hidden in the wool and finally Rachel
delivers the greatest shock of all: that Isabel has gone to
Boreray. These shocks build up to the climax of the play and
provide a crucial turning point in Aneas's development. He is
stunned and made to suffer real anguish, reaching his lowest
emotional point in the play, but he also begins to see how
blind he has been and to doubt many of his certainties. Thus
he prepares himself to accept the very changed Isabel who
returns from Boreray and to face the consequences of her
sending the letter.

Act Two, Scene Five
The next scene is shorter still and Glover does not keep the
audience waiting for Isabel's return, but instead moves on

immediately to it. Just as she did not include a wedding scene earlier, she focuses on the effect Boreray has had on Isabel, rather than the experience itself. Another type of drama or film might have kept us waiting in order to increase the suspense at this point, whereas moving immediately to Isabel's return in the very next scene highlights how dramatically Isabel's character has changed. It also helps to stress the urgency with which events are now moving, as Aneas and Isabel must now leave the island immediately.

Notice too how the stage directions and the dialogue help us to see Isabel's conflicting emotions at the start of this scene. Aneas hurries onstage with Isabel having been told to follow him straight from the boat, but she follows 'reluctantly' and we are told that 'she is caught between the guilt of her disobedient departure for Boreray and the exhilaration of her adventures there' and also 'she has come to realise – perversely, in his absence – her affection for Aneas'. The choice of the word 'perversely' clearly signals that Isabel should feel that this is somehow wrong, but that she has been surprised by her own feelings of affection for him when he does not really deserve it. Isabel babbles on, using very short, incomplete or hyphenated sentences, showing how exhilarated she still is and how much she 'loved being on Boreray' and how on the cliffs she 'could have flown'.

Indeed, the actress must suggest by her manner, pace and tone of voice at this point that she feels she is still 'flying', but at the same time indicate that her nervous chatter is trying to cover her uncertainty about what she should do or say and about how Aneas will react. Although she 'doesn't know how to apologise for going off to Boreray', we are told how she 'falters' twice and when she says 'I led the psalms, night and morning', she says this 'contritely', as if she feels a bit guilty and is trying to placate him.

Considering how stunned Aneas was at the end of the previous scene, and the fact that we immediately see him hurrying onstage followed by Isabel, we are expecting Aneas to be very angry with her for disobeying him. At first she thinks he has not forgiven her, as he hardly says anything, partly because he cannot get a word in, and so, when he approaches her to embrace her, she is 'quite alarmed', but he is simply relieved and thankful that she is safe and caresses her to show his love for her. Yet, while he is clearly thankful and seems to be forgiving, we see from the way he talks to her that, although his 'manner shows' that he forgives her, 'his words do not' and he uses the word 'deceived', repeating the word 'twice' for emphasis, though he is now more concerned about the arrival of the Steward and the trouble they are now in.

Notice the use of the antithetical question and answer that does not answer her question: 'It will do her no good now, the letter? It will do us great harm'. His failure to reply directly to her question (as the answer is obvious) immediately emphasises the effect her actions will now have on them. They will be immediately sent back to Edinburgh in disgrace for causing trouble for his employers. Aneas also fears that he will never get 'a living' now and he seems almost resigned to becoming a 'stickit' minister. Yet in spite of the fact that he could suffer a great deal because of it, he now feels that Isabel was 'right', though 'rash' and 'misguided', to send the letter and she has in fact 'done less wrong [...] far less wrong' than he has. In addition he will do what he can on Rachel's behalf when he gets back to Edinburgh, although they are 'small folk' in comparison with the Granges and Lovats who 'prowl and prosper', like big powerful predatory cats. In other words it will be very difficult, it will not do Aneas's career any good and it could even be dangerous.

In spite of that, what is now more important to him is simply 'his beloved wife', his last words in the play, which stress, in their simplicity, that he feels he has at last truly earned Isabel's respect, love and devotion. Their relationship has been saved by finding a new bond of respect, understanding and enduring love for each other as result of their redeeming experience on Hirta.

In contrast to the conscientious but rather self-righteous, judgemental minister, lacking warmth, compassion and understanding of women in particular, Aneas develops a new humility from living among genuinely good people who share a communal, caring way of life, without a church or minister. He feels that their real faith and kindness have made him a priest which he 'hardly was before', meaning he can now truly care for his flock, whereas previously he was like many religious people who do not practise the important aspects of their faith, but instead concentrate on the outward trappings of religious devotion and piety. This, along with the influence of the women, has helped him to become more understanding of his own wife and more sympathetic towards Rachel, the person most in need of his help. At the end, he is prepared to put his principles before his career to do what little he can to fight injustice and cruelty.

It is finally through this new humility, humanity and integrity that Aneas earns the respect, love and forgiveness of a genuinely good woman, his wife, Isabel, who has come a long way from the despairing innocent she was when she first landed on Hirta. Isabel has finally found the 'adventure' she craved on escaping from the confines of her sheltered and very restricted Edinburgh life, but not quite in the way she could have imagined. In Act One, Scene Two, Rachel asks Isabel, 'don't you love to wear a mask?' and later in the same scene Isabel tells Aneas that she has never 'gone abroad in a mask' (i.e. gone out wearing one). While this is meant to show her lack of experience of the city's sophisticated fashions, it also symbolises her lack of pretence, her inability to conceal anything, in short her openness, honesty and sincerity. These qualities, along with a genuinely selfless and warm-hearted nature, which helped her to cope with bringing up her uncle's children, have made it difficult for her to ignore Rachel's plea for help.

We could see Rachel as something of a catalyst in terms of her influence on Isabel, yet at the same time, Isabel's previously hidden rebellious impulses have risen to the surface in following Rachel's un-ladylike advice. Ironically this helps her to stand up to Rachel and then finally disobey her husband, thereby allowing her to enjoy the friendship, freedom and fun she enjoys with the women on Boreray. She returns a stronger, wiser, more mature woman who can stand up for herself while also caring about others, something she has seen in action in everyday life in this apparently primitive, communal society where love is cherished and celebrated and women play an equal part with men, respecting and supporting each other on a precarious, sometimes dangerous, but beautiful island that sustains and reveres all that is best in people and life.

Act Two, Scene Six

Ending the play with this final very short scene, instead of the previous one featuring Aneas and Isabel, focuses attention back onto the tragic figure of Rachel. Rachel is doomed to remain a prisoner, to continue to the end of her days dreaming of escape, still writing her pathetic letters, with no pen or paper, no one to deliver them, and no one to listen other than Oona, endlessly patient, kindly and uncomplaining, but still her prison guard. Glover highlights the tragic futility of her situation by having her write imaginary letters, having Oona trying to mend her broken straw chair and by having her revert to her 'society tone' as the play closes, still pretending she is an aristocrat.

We move away from the focus on love restored of the previous scene and return to the theme of love lost and betrayed and the bitter experience of a woman warped by a poisonous relationship, cruelly separated from her family, now abandoned on a remote rocky island as a madwoman, because she raged against her husband's infidelities and hypocrisies. Thus the ending increases our sympathy for the trapped, tragic figure, driven mad by her cruel treatment at the hands of powerful men and now destined to spend her remaining days here, shrunken, frailer and suffering not only emotionally and mentally but also physically from leg ulcers and possibly breast cancer.

At the end we also see Oona mending the chair, still showing kindness and consideration towards the 'lady' who has treated her very disdainfully. She says nothing and sits 'at a distance' 'watching over her', but in her usual patient manner she is repairing the flimsy straw chair to comfort Rachel because she knows how important it is to her and the charade she maintains. Yet while Oona can repair the chair, she cannot repair the damage done to Rachel, as this is something beyond the healing power of her kindness and sympathy.

On the one hand, the mood of the ending is partly one of cautious affirmation or even optimism as two people discover the life enhancing power of genuine, enduring love, and grow stronger and wiser as a result of their time on the island; but, on the other hand, it is also quite bitter, dark and sad. Although love is restored between the minister and his 'beloved wife', they will probably suffer from Isabel trying to help Rachel (as the real minister, Roderick MacLennan, in fact did) and their future is at the mercy of powers and forces beyond their control, while Rachel is left on her rocky prison, broken in spirit and suffering greatly.

11. IMAGERY AND SYMBOLISM

As in *Bondagers*, Glover deploys song, music and movement to express her ideas, while imagery and symbolism are again used to convey deeper levels of meaning. We have already discussed several examples of the latter, such as the clothing imagery, the wearing of masks and the symbolism of the skua in Act One, Scene Four, but there is also some other revealing imagery and symbolism in this scene. While Isabel is 'safely defiant' in keeping the lamp on, since Aneas is too sleepy to notice, it is still an act of defiance, albeit a very timid one. It is only when he is sound asleep that she confides in Rachel, something he would certainly see not just as an act of defiance, but almost unforgivable betrayal. While he is asleep she is also imagining things he would certainly not approve of, especially her fantasy about the scaly snake, associated in Judaic–Christian mythology with the serpent in the Garden of Eden and, since Aneas, like Adam, is asleep, Rachel could be seen as the devil tempting Eve with knowledge of the forbidden fruit.

However, in Celtic mythology the snake is linked to fertility and wisdom (before later religions associated sex with sin and guilt) and the scaly snake, with its phallic connotations, is clearly associated with procreation. The stone bed covered in moss, instead of feathers, obviously suggests the coldness and sterility in their relationship, the absence of any physical warmth and love in a marriage that has not yet been consummated. Thus Aneas is linked metaphorically at this point to darkness and coldness, lack of human warmth and vitality, whereas Isabel is linked to a desire for light, warmth and love. It is also during her conversation with Rachel that she sees the light in more ways than one and by the end of the scene it is dawn and they see the sail on the horizon, which signals multiple wedding celebrations, fertility, new life and hope for the future, perhaps for Isabel as well as the islanders.

In Act Two, Scene Three, Isabel and Rachel's fight over the chair, Isabel's attempt to catch the boat and her rescue from the waves (which we learn about in the next scene) all have important symbolic significance. Since Rachel reclaims the chair from the minister's house at the start and pathetically clings to it as a symbol of her social superiority, Isabel grabbing it and threatening to throw it over the edge shows us that Isabel is now standing up to the aristocratic Rachel, but it could also represent how she is now ready to challenge the conventions of the world she has come from and the authority of those she is conditioned to accept as her superiors. Although we are told she is 'out of her depth' in fighting with Rachel who is 'fiercely professional', and Isabel lets go of the chair, it is Rachel who ends up on her back and has to crawl back to the chair. This suggests an upset in more ways than one: a possible shift of power, even if Isabel offers to mend it, while the fight also clearly highlights Isabel's new spirit of rebellion and determination not to accept other people's expectations and estimations of her.

Rachel's commentary on Isabel running to catch the boat not only shows her changing perception of Isabel but also charts the progress of Isabel's character in the play as a whole:

> RACHEL: It's a long way down! You'll never make it! (…)
> By God but you might!

She almost leaves it too late and takes a very big risk, but does succeed in her 'adventure' against all expectations, with a little help from her friends. As we learn from Rachel in the next scene, Isabel jumped and landed in the water, but was 'lifted' from the waves by the women, a powerful symbol of rescue and rebirth, a sort of baptism into a new life and a new identity, thanks to the women of this island, in preparation for the transformation that she is undergoing and which we will see completed on her return from Boreray. Notice the very positive connotations of 'lifted' as opposed to 'pulled', implying much more than just a physical rescue from drowning, more an uplifting in a personal sense, almost a spiritual salvation or redemption.

The straw chair, the main prop out of the few used, is the central symbol in the play, focusing our minds on Rachel and her problems. She haughtily reclaims it at the start, asserting her social superiority over the minister as she believes she is 'the highest born' person on the island, a distinction that is ironically meaningless in the communal, classless society of Hirta. She almost clings to it as a symbol of her former status, but in fact it really shows how far she has fallen. A straw chair is flimsy and worthless, therefore an effective symbol of empty authority and lost power – a power rooted in the social hierarchy from which she has been banished and which has no relevance here, just like her tattered Edinburgh gown.

However, chairs also have a deeper symbolic significance in the play. Rachel herself reminds us of how the lack of chairs on Hirta contrasts with the house full of expensive chairs she once had in Edinburgh, something she in fact likes to boast about. In addition she also talks about Lord Grange's chair that no one else was allowed to sit on and which contained the hidden drawer with his secret letters, suggesting his deviousness and hypocrisy. Thus chairs are an important recurring symbol of power which also helps to develop the contrast between, on the one hand, the chairless, classless society of Hirta, with its simple lifestyle and positive human values but, on the other, the mercenary, scheming world of the rich and powerful at the heart of a sophisticated Edinburgh society where people love wearing masks, where love is poisoned and betrayed and where women can be disposed of whenever they are no longer of any use and where people can simply disappear if they are causing the powerful to feel 'uncomfortable'. Thus the play's short title cleverly focuses our mind not only on how Rachel clings pointlessly to a lost aristocratic status but also on how chairs eventually symbolise the power, property-owning tyranny and hypocrisy of a corrupt, male dominated society. We can surely infer from this contrast between a primitive island and a 'civilised' society that Glover is not simply talking about eighteenth-century Scotland, but also about the corrupt and hypocritical values of modern wealth-worshipping, class-ridden societies anywhere.

Notice also the use of letter-writing symbolism throughout the play. Oona is in awe of Aneas's ability to turn black marks into words, making it sound like black magic, Rachel is always desperately trying to get her hands on paper and ink, Lord Grange's secret letters were hidden in his chair and Isabel sending Rachel's letter will do Aneas and herself a great deal of harm, while at the end Rachel is left pathetically writing her imaginary letters. All of this suggests the difficulties or dangers involved in trying to communicate with those in power, as Rachel's letters are never delivered or will never be written. No one in authority is listening; she has become a non-person. Yet letters also symbolise the power of the written word, as the secret, hidden or smuggled letters seem to reflect relationships and a society with much to hide. Like the imagery of mask-wearing, so letters also symbolise deceit, danger and evil, something possibly suggested by the 'black marks' on paper that Oona feels she could never learn if she lived 'a hundred thousand years'.

All of this contrasts with the oral communication of the island and its shared culture of stories, songs, psalms and rituals, of communal food gathering and sharing, of betrothal ordeals and the magical celebration of nine weddings at once. This all takes place offstage, but we are shown the dramatic, life-enhancing effect they have on Isabel (her name means 'worshipper of / consecrated to God' in Hebrew), the innocent young wife of the 'stickit' little minister Aneas, whose life is much changed by his travels, like his classical namesake in *The Aeneid*, but unlike Virgil's hero (who forsook his lover, Queen Dido), he continues on his way accompanied by a truly 'beloved wife'.

12. CONCLUSION

In both plays, Glover explores Scottish history from a female perspective, giving voice to exploited or alienated women whose identity has been determined by their domestic or working role or their social status in a hypocritical patriarchal society. Both show women resisting or struggling to change things, but though it may be difficult and the cost high, change is not impossible. The endings may be dark or at least ambivalent, but ultimately there is a cautious optimism about both works, especially in the way Glover portrays women gaining strength and wisdom from each other and in the way she celebrates the positive bonds of human interdependency that are essential to our survival and progress as a species. Both are profoundly Scottish plays but both are universal in their significance, relevance and appeal.

13. FURTHER READING

The Prisoner of St Kilda by Margaret Macaulay (Edinburgh: Luath Press, 2009) which investigates the true story of Lady Grange's abduction and also tells of how the Rev. Roderick MacLennan's career suffered as a consequence of trying to help her. There is an extensive bibliography at the end of the book.

'Lady Grange on St Kilda', a sonnet by Edwin Morgan

Island on the Edge of the World by Charles Maclean (Edinburgh: Canongate, 2006)

The Life and Death of St Kilda by Tom Steele (London: HarperPress, 2011)

St Kilda: Church, Visitors and Natives by Michael Robson (Lewis: Islands Book Trust, 2005)

St Kilda: A Journey to the End of the World by Campbell McCutcheon (Stroud: Amberley Publishing, 2008)

The Truth About St Kilda by Donald Gillies (Edinburgh: John Donald, 2010)

Lightning Source UK Ltd.
Milton Keynes UK
UKHW021848030221
378186UK00007B/290